BLACK LIVES DON'T MATTER

IN AMERICA'S CRIMINAL JUSTICE SYSTEM

A SYSTEM THAT HAS NEVER BEEN FAIR AND
EQUITABLE TO BLACK AND BROWN PEOPLE

TERRY NELSON

NEWMAN SPRINGS PUBLISHING
320 Broad Street
Red Bank, NJ 07701

First originally published by Newman Springs Publishing 2022

ISBN 978-1-63881-119-0 (Paperback)
ISBN 978-1-63881-124-4 (Digital)

Printed in the United States of America

CONTENTS

PREFACE

Blind justice should be defined as a judiciary system that makes a decision based upon evidence presented without an outside influence or predisposition and that the decision is based upon the applicable law(s). It further means that the courts are to be impartial and not biased in their decision-making.

I would like to further define *blind justice* as...

> Given a certain scenario of facts when deciding a case, most reasonable people will come to the same decision.

Well, most people would agree that is just not true. History has shown time and time again that a majority-White jury will get different results in a criminal hearing than a majority-Black jury when given the same set of facts and circumstances, especially when it comes to Black and minority defendants. Based upon my observations and experiences, I just cannot see how blind justice has ever been applicable in our current society.

I am of the opinion that the internet and media (television, radio, newspapers) can definitely affect the outcomes on a judicial decision, which can lead to positive and negative outcomes. I feel that to truly have a blind system of justice, there should never be any facts, theories, or media coverage of any kind to be observed by a judge or jury—be it verbal, written, or audiovisual—prior to a hearing or while a hearing is in progress. Why? Because prejudice is real.

Prejudice is to prejudge a person or incident based on predetermined bias about a person, be it race, sex, sexual orientation, etc. Modern media almost makes it impossible for many criminal activities to be judged on a nonbiased basis. When you are watching someone on television getting arrested for an alleged crime, many people, after seeing the individual and listening to the charges, will have already made the assumption of guilt.

Which brings us to the phrase "innocent until proven guilty," which is a joke. There is no such thing in our current judicial system. As soon as charges are brought against an individual, the individual is then treated as a criminal. They are arrested, charged, and put in jail. Keep in mind that many individuals are falsely accused. Just because a person is charged with a criminal offense does not mean that they are guilty.

Then why are people treated like criminals when they have not been convicted or found guilty of the alleged crime? Those that are fortunate can post bail. Those that are less fortunate have to sit in jail and suffer the serious consequences of a jail environment. Jail can leave scars on innocent individuals for life. While in jail, they can be subjected to mental, verbal, and sexual abuse as well as intolerable living conditions, which no innocent person should have to be subjected to.

My observations and experiences with this judicial and criminal justice system inspired me to write this book. There is no doubt in my mind that the United States Criminal Justice and Judicial System needs to be changed. I have come to the conclusion that our current systems are prejudiced, unfair, and a joke to Black and Brown minorities.

Don't get me wrong; it does work for some. However, it best serves the guilty, not the innocent and/or the White population. It does not effectively serve the Blacks or Brown populations. Based on my life experiences as a Black man living in the United States, I have concluded that our criminal justice system is an injustice to Black and Brown communities. I am of the opinion that the reason the criminal justice system does not work well for the Black and Brown communities is because it was never designed to do so. It was constructed for White people by White people. When this so-called perfect Union was formed, it just was not designed to include Black and Brown people.

The good news is that it can be fixed. The bad news is that it has to be torn down and reconstructed to be fair and inclusive to all. There is absolutely no way that a bandage or training class can fix this severely broken system. The corruption is so widespread and ingrained in our law enforcement institutions that it just cannot be fixed in its current state.

The following is a critical look at our current criminal justice system through a Black man's eyes.

THE ACCUSATION
OF A CRIME

When a person is charged with a crime, it is generally alleged that the person committed the crime. The allegations could be true, false, or assumed. The accused person is arrested, booked, jailed, or bailed (terms and conditions are based on the severity of the alleged crime). The process is the same whether the accused individual admits to the alleged crime or not, which means that the criminal justice system is designed to take the position of the accuser over the individual being accused the majority of the time.

Keep in mind that all people are supposed to be innocent until proven guilty. If this is the case, then why is an accused individual being treated like a criminal before being convicted of the crime in a court of law? We have to ask ourselves, is this fair to the accused as we all know too well that many people are falsely accused? I would estimate that approximately 25 percent of those accused of a crime is falsely accused. How do so many people get falsely accused?

First of all, it is a fact that in most violent crimes where there are witnesses and/or victims, the witnesses or victims cannot properly identify the criminal. It is a known fact that most people cannot correctly identify a criminal during a lineup. This is a major problem that faces our criminal justice system.

Some reasons that victims and witnesses have problems making a positive identification of a criminal may be due to the following:

I would estimate that approximately 50 percent of the general population has poor recall when it comes to identifying an individual. It appears to get worse when it comes to White people's identifying people of color. For some reason, many White people feel that most

Black people look alike. For example, if a White person was a victim of a crime and they know that the criminal was a dark-skinned Black man then, you put that dark-skinned Black man in a lineup with all light-skinned Black men, guess who is going to most likely be chosen as soon as a victim sees the darker-skinned Black man's face.

It is a shame but true. Many people of color get caught in this trap. It can also work the reverse. For example, if witnesses identify a light-skinned Black man as the criminal, by putting one light-skinned black man in a lineup with all dark-skinned Black men, the light-skinned Black man would most likely be chosen whether he committed the crime or not.

The most reasonable explanation for this is that most White people don't look at the features of a Black man as much as they do the skin color. So in many of their minds, if the skin color matches the description, then it must be the person.

Generally, people are more correctly identifiable when they have what I like to call standout features such as

- a visible tattoo
- an eye color that is unique to a particular race such as a Black person with green, blue, or hazel eyes
- a Black person with blond or red hair
- an unusually shaped head
- being very tall or very short
- being very skinny or extremely obese
- a unique voice pitch (extremely higher or lower than normal)
- a speech impediment
- an unusual nose or mouth feature
- a dental stand-out feature such as broken teeth, stained teeth, gold teeth, perfect teeth, gaped teeth, etc.
- a unique shape or structure of facial hairs

Those are some of the characteristics that could assist in correctly identifying a suspect. As a victim, people should always try to focus on something that would make the criminal stand out, something that if you saw that person again, you would easily be able to identify them (unless the person had a twin or that the likeness is so great that the majority of people would not be able to recognize or identify the difference).

To be fair, identification is a serious problem regardless of race or sex. I am sure that many people have heard people say, "I can't remember the name, but I remember the face, or I can remember the face but can't recall the name." I feel that most people fall into one of these categories.

I personally fall in the category of not remembering names but have excellent facial recall. Once, I was a victim of a robbery. While working at a grocery store, two armed men came in with scarfs covering their faces. They robbed the store by taking money from the cash registrar, and they took any/all jewelry that the store employees were wearing. They took a class ring and a watch from me. One was armed with a handgun and the other with a sawed-off shotgun.

The police caught the two robbers later that evening after they attempted to rob another local grocery store. We (the victims) were notified by local police that two robbery suspects had been caught while attempting to rob another store and that they were in police custody.

We (the victims) were invited down to the police station and asked to identify the two robbery suspects out of a lineup. The police had two different lineups, each consisting of four guys. There were three of us that were victimized by the robbery. I was the only one that correctly identified both robbery suspects. Both of the other two robbery victims picked the same two robbery suspects incorrectly. I was told by the police officers that I correctly identified the two robbery suspects and was then shown the contents of the robbery, which included my class ring and watch.

I was really shocked that the other two store robbery victims were unable to correctly identify the actual robbers. One police officer stated that he was quite surprised that I was able to make a positive identification because of the fact that both men were wearing scarfs covering half of their faces at the time of the store robbery. To me, it was easy because all the men in the lineup had scarves on covering the lower portion of their faces. I was able to specifically remember their eyes, head, and body structure.

After that incident, I began to realize that few people have superior identification recall skills, and I am possibly one of them. But what bothered me most about this situation was that the other two store robbery victims were willing to make sworn statements that the two people that they picked out of the police lineup were the store robbers. They were both willing to convict two people of a crime that they were innocent of. To make matters worse, both robbery victims were 100 percent sure that they had picked the right two robbers. If people are not sure when picking out an alleged criminal, they need to express their uncertainty at that time.

Some of the following are factors involved in assisting the blocking of victims and witnesses from expressing any uncertainty when picking people out of a lineup.

1. Police or law enforcement agencies assisting people during the lineup procedure. Oftentimes, law enforcement agencies offer assistance to help build a case against an alleged criminal. They will offer their advice to the victim or witness. Sometimes, they use what I refer to as unethical tactics, such as pressuring victims or witnesses to say that they positively identified the person when the victim or witness is really not sure. Often, the victim or witness will pick two people out of a lineup. Because the victim or witness is not 100 percent sure, the victim or witness will state that they feel it is one or the other. Then law enforcement officials will put pressure on the victim or witness to pick one.

   Sometimes, the person picked by the victim or witness is not the right one. Law enforcement officials often (for whatever reason) feel that a certain person in the lineup is the guilty person. This could be from the person's past criminal history, evidence collected during the investigation, or through prior questioning of the individual being accused. Far too many times, law enforcement officials build a case on their personal beliefs and suspicions. Needless to say, they are not always right. This seems to especially be true when it comes to investigating and charging Blacks and people of color.

2. Most Black and Brown people look alike to most non-Black and minority accusers, especially when the accuser is White or of a different race. For some reason, people seem to do better identifying suspects of their own race, which means Whites will do better at identifying White criminals, Blacks will do better at identifying Black criminals, Hispanics with do better at identifying Hispanic criminals, etc.

3. When people have been a victim of a crime, they often are compelled to find someone guilty of that crime. This, in turn, makes it easier to put the blame on an innocent person. For example, if a person robbed by a Black man is picking a person out of a lineup, it is easy to just say that this person looks close to the robber, so it must be him.

Clearly, there is not much that can be done to prevent the many cases of false identification that occur. However, there should be better rules and policies in place to help minimize the devastation of false identification. I suggest some or all of the following to assist in making a better more fair process for identifying suspected criminals:

First of all, I feel the people that bring charges against a person for a criminal offense should be explained all the possible consequences for making a false identification. Accusers and witnesses need to know that if they wrongly accused a person of a crime, it could have devastating effects on that person's life as well as on his or her future. This may sound harsh, but I feel that people making a positive criminal identification, and if it turns out that the identification was wrong, then those accusers need to sustain some type of accountability. It could be in the form of cash, community service, jail, or some combination thereof.

Far too many times, false accusations cause mental trauma, family breakups as well as wrongful jail time. Speaking of jail time; jail is no picnic. The possible mistreatment from other inmates, deplorable living conditions, and mental trauma that a jail environment may cause can have irreversible effects on a person. Jail is something that no innocent person should ever have to endure.

Moreover, I feel that no one should ever be held in jail prior to being found guilty of a crime. There needs to be some type of alternative to jail for people awaiting a trial. The only exception should be if there is overwhelming evidence that a person is guilty of a crime. Jail should always be a last alternative. More efforts should be focused on a monitoring system. With modern technology, it would be easy to place electronic monitors on or within a person's body. This way a person can be tracked and monitored until trial and/or sentencing.

Granted, there will be some problems with this procedure, as there are with all programs, but if society really cares about innocent people's rights and/or freedom, society has to start looking at some form of alternative as to how we deal with accused criminals up until they are found guilty of a crime.

What many people are not aware of is that prison can have a very negative impact on its habitants. It can turn good people bad. Some inmates are jumped on, raped, harassed, and/or shamed. Getting over that experience is not easy, and some people never get over it. Many people may want to get back at the system after getting released from jail, especially when they are found innocent of the alleged charges. What often happens is that a noncriminal is made into a criminal.

I equate being in prison as similar to being in a war. The situations that a person may encounter can be devastating. Some people are able to rehabilitate, and some are not; some can be helped with counseling, and some cannot. So what happens to those who cannot get over the jail experience?

- Some turn to alcohol and/or drugs.
- Some physically and/or mentally abuse family members or other members of the general population.
- Some resort to violence and/or violent behavior.
- Some turn against the system and/or give up all trust.
- Some may commit suicide or lose their will/desire to live.

Our justice system has got to learn how to respect the rights of all people and realize that a criminal is not a criminal until convicted of a crime. Allegations are not convictions. This practice of treating an alleged criminal as a convicted criminal has to stop.

There was recently a case in Chicago, Jussie Smollett. Smollett reported to the Chicago Police Department that he had been assaulted physically and verbally by his attackers. Smollett alleged he had been a victim of a hate crime to the Chicago Police Department. After investigating the matter, the Chicago Police Department came to the decision that Jessie's claims were untrue and concluded that Jessie made the whole incident up.

There was a serious problem with the Chicago Police Department's handling of this case for the following reasons:

First of all, the police chief had no business whatsoever to go on national television to discuss any details on the case as the case was still active and pending a court hearing to determine Smollett's innocence or guilt. It was not the job of the Chicago Police Department to determine Smollett's innocence or guilt. This police chief took upon himself to discuss his findings based on the evidence he had at hand and the statement of the two suspected accusers to be accurate and made the determination that the whole incident was fabricated by Smollett.

This is a serious violation of protocol. It is not up to a police department to be the judge and/or jury. In this case, the only procedure that the police department was to do was process the alleged charge; interview all parties concerned, including witness statements; and present the findings to the judicial system. There is that old saying: "everything is not always as it appears." Keeping this in mind, no one directly involved with the investigation of a case should ever publically discuss or disclose their findings to the general public, especially while a case is on-going.

Even though the Chicago Police investigation appeared to paint a different picture than the one that Smollett had presented, this still does not mean that the Chicago Police Department came to the right conclusion. Moreover, it appears that all law enforcement agencies have lost their sense of purpose. A law enforcement agency's function in a criminal case is to investigate, gather information, and report their findings to the judicial system. Then it is the judicial systems responsibility to review the findings and information obtained by the law enforcement agency and determine whether to proceed to a trial.

Far too often, the police departments are being the judge and the jury in the cases that they are investigating. *This practice needs to cease.* There would be far less problems if every law enforcement agency does exactly what they were designed to do.

We have seen many cases that have gone unsolved because the law enforcement agency go after who they feel is guilty while ignoring all other leads and/or possibilities. Which, in turn, results in the wrong person being charged or convicted while the guilty person gets away with the criminal act.

This rush to judgment needs to stop. It is better to take the time and get everything right even if all investigating details lead to a dead end. Every effort needs to be focused on getting the right person that committed the crime and not just making a person guilty to close a case.

Keep in mind that law enforcement officials get promotions, raises, and all kinds of other accolades for closing cases with a suspect. The bigger picture is that many of these law enforcement officials will do anything to get the case closed. They will falsely charge an innocent person even when they know that the evidence collected shows a greater possibility of his or her innocence. Why? Open cases do not look good for any law enforcement agency or department. Having too many open cases has the perception of incompetence. For the life of me, I could never understand how any agency could charge a person with a crime that they know the person did not commit. How could anyone knowingly charge an innocent person while the guilty person is still out there free.

Far too many people have been a victim of these procedures, and it needs to stop. People need to come to the realization that not all criminals are going to be caught. Some criminal investigations may take years to solve. No matter what, it is always better to have the right person that committed a crime than to have the wrong person charged and/or convicted of a crime. The main focus should always be on getting the right person. All law enforcement agencies have to refocus their mission and put the greatest emphasis on doing the right thing.

This is the very reason why so many Blacks and minorities have very little faith in the integrity of our law enforcement officials. Blacks and minorities know that they have a greater possibility of being charged with a crime when they are innocent, primarily because many police departments are looking to make someone guilty so that they can close an open case.

Getting back to the Smollett case, the Chicago Police Department interviewed two men (brothers). The two brothers told the police that Smollett paid them to stage an attack on him and making it appear to be racially motivated. The Chicago Police obtained video from a store showing the brothers purchasing materials that appeared to be used in the attack on Smollett. The brothers also produced a copy of a check that they said Smollett paid them for the staged attack. The check was for a large sum of money, approximately ten thousand dollars.

The problem with this situation was that the Chicago Police Department totally believed the two brothers. This is not to say that the brothers were right or wrong. However, Smollett never admitted his involvement with the incident. Throughout the entire investigation, Smollett maintained that he had no direct involvement in the incident.

Needless to say, the Chicago Police Department closed the investigation with the belief that the two brother's version of the incident was correct. These investigative results could be a problem for the following reasons:

Just because the Chicago Police Department got two stories from the brothers compared against the one from Smollett, that does not mean that the brothers were telling the truth. The brothers left the United States shortly after the incident and were interviewed by the Chicago Police Department approximately a couple of weeks after they returned to the United States, which means they had plenty of time to coordinate a story together.

After reviewing the case details and investigation report, the Cook County Attorney's Office decided not to press charges against Smollett. After the charges were dropped, Smollett had a press conference maintaining his innocence. Smollett reaffirmed that his detailed version of events as he reported were true and criticized the Chicago Police Department for their one-sided conclusion of events. Most likely, Smollett was upset because the Chicago Police Department totally discounted his version of events.

Why did the Cook County Attorney's Office dismiss the charges? I am fairly sure that some of the following was considered in their reasoning:

- The chief of police went on TV and social media criticizing Smollett and discounting Smollett's statement of events.
- The chief of police insisted that Jessie was the mastermind of the attack. He based his entire decision on the statements and evidence provided by the brothers.
- The chief of police indicated that there was no need to investigate the matter further because he was certain that his investigation findings were correct.

What the chief of police did was wrong and totally out of order. He is entitled to his belief and/or opinion; however, it does not mean that his investigation leading to his decision was not flawed. First of all, the police obtained video footage of the brothers purchasing supplies that were used in committing the attack against Smollett. I wonder if it ever occurred to the chief of police that the brothers could have purchased the materials to give to someone else to commit the crime against Smollett.

Secondly, the brother's provided a copy of a cashed check that was paid to them by Smollett. The check was a large check, approximately ten thousand dollars. However, all of the following would need to be taken into consideration before just coming to the conclusion that the check had to be for payment of a staged crime. The check that Smollett gave the brothers could have been for many other reasons such as a drug debt, personal training expenses owed for past or future personal training services (Smollett stated that one of the brothers was his personal gym training instructor), or it could have been for some type of blackmail.

When Smollett was questioned about the brothers' statements of events, Smollett denied any involvement in the attack incident. Smollett also admitted to having a sexual encounter with one of the brothers.

There was a lot of inconsistent evidence presented in this case. The brothers admitted that they committed the attack on Smollett. However, the reason was never crystal clear. The brothers provided one sequence of events, and Smollett provided another.

Technically, the police did their job by finding the attackers. They had an admission and two different sequences of events. The police department's job regarding the case should have been done at that point. The file should have been turned over to the county attorneys for further review. This case clearly shows how law enforcement agencies draw conclusions based on limited information and facts. Oftentimes, police or law enforcement agencies draw conclusions based on incomplete information.

Any good investigator is aware that when there are two totally separate accounts of an incident, especially when the variation of events is entirely different, a more detailed investigation is required to determine the appropriate and correct sequence of events. Just because the investigative findings appear to be correct during an investigation does not mean that they are indeed correct.

I find that this type of rush to judgment occurs far too often, and the effects of such a rush to judgment can be devastating. At best, the chief of police should have only stated that their findings showed huge discrepancies in Jessie's sequence of events when compared with the brother's sequence of events. That is why there are lawyers, judges, and juries so that all evidence is reviewed and to point out any flaws or discrepancies in the investigative process.

One of the biggest problems with law enforcement agencies is that they often overstep their bounds. If they did exactly what they were created to do, it would make for a far better criminal justice system. There are many factors involved in an investigation, including the following:

- Was the investigation fair and unbiased?
- Was the investigation thorough?
- Was all contradicting information presented and investigated?
- Was there any evidence that showed their findings could be flawed?
- Were the investigators truthful and fair in reporting their findings?

All the above factors are so very important and are the main reason why many cases are won or lost.

What many people don't understand is that there is a big problem with integrity. People lie far more than they tell the truth. This is true for the investigators, the victims, the witnesses, and the accused.

Once the law enforcement agency completes its investigation, it should be turned over to the legal justice system for review and recommendation of charges. Once the legal justice system reviews the law enforcement investigation, it is up to the legal justice system to proceed further. If the legal justice system has decided not to proceed further, the matter is closed. It is not up to the investigating law enforcement agency to dispute the legal justice system's actions. The lawyers looking over cases oftentimes see flaws that the law enforcement agency did not see or that they overlooked.

Sometimes, even if the law enforcement agency's investigation is solid, the legal justice system will decide not to pursue a matter because it may be in the best interest not to do so. In such cases, it does not mean that a person is innocent or guilty; it just means that for some reason the legal justice system does not feel that it is in the best interest to go forward. It could be due to costs, negative publicity, or a very difficult case to win based on the facts that were presented. Whatever the reason, it does not afford the opportunity for a chief of police to get on national TV and voice his opinion or discuss details of the case.

Keep in mind that the police investigation had not been proven to be the actual account of events. Going on national TV and discussing his beliefs and findings was out of order. What the chief of police failed to realize was that his five minutes of fame could have cost the city of Chicago millions of dollars in lawsuits if his findings and beliefs were proven to be incorrect. Law enforcement agencies have to learn to realize that their findings are just findings. As we all know, findings don't always turn out to be the truth.

I feel that law enforcement agencies should concentrate on getting all the facts right, presenting all evidence found, and have the highest integrity in their reporting. Then they need to realize that their job is done. They need to learn how to keep their personal feelings out of investigations and fully concentrate on fact finding. Once they finish their investigation, they have to include all evidence found or obtained, then let the legal justice system do its job.

Far too often, law enforcement officials leave out information or include selective information in their reporting. *This practice needs to stop immediately.* Anyone found guilty of such practices should be terminated, fined, and/or sentenced to prison.

People wonder why Blacks and other minorities don't trust our law enforcement agencies. It is because the system lacks integrity. If the investigators don't like a person or feel a person is guilty, instead of looking for the truth, they set out to build a case of guilt on innocent people.

The biggest problem with our law enforcement agencies is that they lie more than the criminals that they are trying to convict. They will lie about the evidence, the investigation, and their findings. Law enforcement officials need to be held accountable, just like everybody else. If they are caught lying or willfully making false representations, they too should be held accountable. Everybody deserves a truthful investigation, even if the investigation does not produce the results that the investigators were hoping for or thought that it should.

Everybody is aware that law enforcement officers have a code of silence. Many officers will lie or distort facts to protect their own. There will never be any credibility in the law enforcement agencies until this practice stops. *If you see something, say something*; this has to apply to everyone.

I really believe if people could trust law enforcement to do the right thing that they, in turn, will also do the right thing, at least for the most part. I have talked to many police officers, and most feel that the biggest problem that they face is solving criminal cases is the lack of cooperation from the general public. It does not take a rocket scientist to understand that you get what you give. Historically, there has been a big mistrust of law enforcement officers with the general public. The only way to establish trust with the general public going forward is *law enforcement officers have to start doing the right thing.*

The true mission of law enforcement should be to protect the people that they serve and not just to protect their own. For the life of me, I could never understand why law enforcement officers fraudulently present evidence to convict an innocent person. In recent years, body cams and people recording incidents while they are happening is bringing light to just how rotten that some of our law enforcement officials really are.

Moreover, a bigger problem is that the good law enforcement officials are working with the rotten ones. However, it is rare that they will go against the rotten ones. When put on the spot, even many of the good law enforcement officers will lie and support their fellow officer's mistruths. I wonder why?

Well, what would be the consequences for an officer reporting that another officer has lied and falsified his reporting? This most likely would cause a rift in the department, and the officer that refuses to go along with a lying officer's report would be looked at as a rat. The officer telling the truth would probably be threatened and could not trust the department to treat him fairly going forward, nor could he trust the other officers to have his back when working dangerous missions.

Personally, I believe that this is a major factor in police suicides. They see things but feel that they cannot go against the system for fear of retaliation, which could jeopardize their own personal safety.

Under the current law enforcement officer's working conditions, only a limited number of people can work successfully in this environment. A person such as myself could never survive under these circumstances. I could never live with watching a fellow officer take the life of an innocent person for no reason or to charge a person of a criminal offense when I know that the person is innocent. I would not be able to support those injustice activities, especially when most of the injustices are against my own race.

I really feel that the culture of many police departments is so bad that they are just not repairable under the current circumstances, which means that the only way to fix the current police department situation is to start over from the ground up. A new culture has to be established. The existing culture has been deeply embedded in the current law enforcement structure.

I personally feel that taking a class or doing some retraining is just not good enough to correct the current corruption that exists. A new law enforcement ethic has to be established. From day one, police have to be trained that all lives matter exactly the same. All future police have to have a total regard for all human life. They have to understand that any disregard for human life will result in severe consequences—up to and including termination, jail time, disciplinary action, and/or fines/fees. A new law structure has to reward police officers that do the right thing no matter what the right thing may be.

Right now, the current system only rewards a criminal law enforcement structure. Can you imagine how many police officers have been promoted or received additional compensation for lies and/or false convictions?

The current law enforcement department's integrity has been devastating and cannot continue. It is obvious that Black and Brown people have suffered the most under the corrupt policing policies. Under the current system, it is impossible to be a good police officer. There are no rewards whatsoever for exposing corruption within the system. Even if a police officer wanted to, the consequences would be devastating. No system can be good if it does not reward truth, honesty, or integrity.

I firmly believe that only when a police department values the truth, honesty, integrity, and fairness will it make a better place for all police officers. Right now, only the bad ones are protected under the current system.

Can you imagine having to work every day with a person whom you know doesn't respect human life and will kill Black and Brown people for no valid moral reason at all, and you can't say or do anything about it? That is a terrible feeling, and good people would not be able to thrive under such circumstances.

This is a very serious matter and *definitely* needs attention. The current police departments have to be restructured. Truth, honesty, and integrity has to be the primary focus going forward. The good police have to be protected, rewarded, and highly encouraged to do the right thing. Bad law enforcement officers have got to start being held accountable for their actions.

It is ironic that law enforcement officers are always pleading to the community for people to come forward and help them solve a crime. That is easy to say but not that easy to do, especially when police are consistently lying, killing, and mistreating the public that they serve. Far too often, when it comes to the Black and Brown communities, the White police officers are quick to shoot or kill a Black male.

I have spoken to many police officers regarding this matter, and the common response is that "we are trained to shoot to kill." If this is indeed the case, this needs to be changed. Going forward, police officers need to be trained that pulling a trigger will always be the last resort.

In a recent Chicago police officer's killing of a Black male, the other officers on the scene were asked by media and attorneys why the male victim could not have been Tased instead of being shot sixteen times. The response was that none of the police officers on the scene had any Tasers. To me, that is a disgrace and shows little to no effort on even wanting to save a human life. Police have to learn how to defuse situations and to make every effort to not escalate a situation and making it life threatening.

Just to show how times have changed, in the 1960s and 1970s, as a young black male teenager, we ran from the police all the time. Chicago police officers rarely shot at anyone not suspected of committing a felony crime. Oftentimes, they would chase the people running, and if they caught them, they would rough them up with a nightstick or with their fists. Today, a Black male better not run from a police officer; whether he committed a crime or not, he will most likely get shot.

Police today need to understand that people will run when they are scared (and many Black and Brown people are scared of police due to mistrust). However, just because someone runs does not mean that they are guilty of a crime. I feel that police officers should never shoot at anyone just because the person is running and fail to stop at a law enforcement officer's command, unless the person running has been observed committing a crime or criminal act.

Currently, the general public has so much distrust with police departments, that it would be next to impossible to change its current perception without some type of massive overhaul. For example, there was recently a case in Kentucky where the police had a no-knock search warrant. They went to the home of Breonna Taylor on an evening sometime after midnight. When they got there, they kicked the door down. During the process, Breonna and her boyfriend were in the house (most likely sleeping at that hour).

The boyfriend had a gun (he was legally licensed to carry and possess a gun). He shot at the officers when he was awakened by the door being kicked in. One of the police officers was shot, and the police department stated that the bullet that shot the officer came from the boyfriend's gun. The police officers shot many rounds of bullets (supposedly after being shot at by the boyfriend). Breonna was shot six times and killed during the police no-knock search.

A no-knock search is when police officers are granted permission to search a residence by a judge. The officers are allowed to break into the residence without having to identify themselves. Needless to say, this type of search can be extremely dangerous in that people inside a home have the legal right to protect their home as well as their lives.

After the incident was over, the police arrested the boyfriend for shooting at and injuring a police officer. The police also claimed that they identified themselves as police officers prior to kicking the door in. The boyfriend claims that he was awakened to sounds of someone kicking the door in and feared for his life. He grabbed his weapon and shot one time when the door was kicked open. It was also documented that he called 911 during the process.

The first time that neighbors in the building were interviewed, all neighbors stated that they did not hear anyone identify themselves as police officers doing the no-knock warrant. Then it was later brought up during additional questioning of the neighbors that one of the neighbors changed his original story, now stating that he did hear the police officers identify themselves as police officers prior to kicking the door in.

None of the police officers were charged with the murder of Breonna Taylor. They stated that once they were fired upon, they had the legal right to fire back, which is in fact true. However, one has to carefully examine this situation. First of all, it is hard to understand why they would have conducted a no-knock warrant at the hour that they did (after midnight). If the purpose was not for a life-threatening reason, I can see no reason to do such a search at that hour, unless there were other mitigating circumstances, which appears not to be a factor in this case.

Secondly, I find the police officers' account of events questionable because it is a fact that most police officers do not do anything that they are not required to do. Meaning, if they were not required to knock on the door and identify themselves as police officers, they most likely did not. Most police are just not going to extend people a courtesy that they don't have to.

Third, the boyfriend only fired one shot, which, to me, indicates that once he realized it was the police, he did not fire additional shots.

Fourth, the boyfriend called 911. If he knew it was police kicking the door in, there is a great possibility that he would not have called 911 to report the incident. What would be the purpose?

Fifth, even if the police officers did identify themselves as police officers prior to kicking the door in, it is a great possibility that the people in the apartment were asleep and may not have heard the identification, especially if it was only called out once.

The worst part about the whole incident is that the person that they were looking for was not even in the apartment.

Everyone reading this should view this situation as if they were in the same shoes as the people who were in the apartment. I am not a violent person. Under normal circumstances, I would never even think about shooting anyone. However, if someone was kicking my door down in the middle of the night for no apparent reason, I would most likely shoot through the door. I probably would not even ask who it is because I would feel that I am in a life-threatening situation.

Furthermore, I would be willing to bet that if the shoe was on the other foot and any of those involved police officers were in the same situation, they would do the same thing. If someone was kicking their door down and they had no knowledge it was police officers, they would shoot to protect themselves as well. To add insult to injury, none of the police officers had on body cameras rolling to back up their story.

On this day, an innocent person died for no reason. There is absolutely no reason that this incident should have occurred in the manner that it did. Knowing the possible dangers of such a search, it would have made more sense that they would have conducted the no-knock warrant at a more decent hour.

They could have surrounded the front and back of the building and granted the people inside a reasonable time to come to the door. A little better planning and a regard for human life would have saved a human life. It is a miracle that the boyfriend did not lose his life as well. Almost anybody who has a weapon for home protection who is placed in a similar situation will most likely result in the same outcome. Somebody is going to get shot, and somebody is most likely going to get killed.

With that said, police should never kick in a door without clearly identifying who they are as well as their intentions. This clearly was not a life-and-death situation until the police made it one. If the police officers really cared about possible loss of life under those circumstances, would it have not been unreasonable to consistently announce that they are police officers with a legal search warrant and request that anyone inside must have their hands up when police enter the property?

Search warrants are a real danger to the general public. People have the right to protect their home and their privacy. In the future, law enforcement agencies have to learn how to better deal with search warrants. If handled properly and with some reasonable caution, it would minimize injuries and possible loss of life. It just takes a little bit of respect for human life and reasonable care.

It is questionable as to whether the police officers told the truth in their summary of events. I seriously doubt that the police gave a credible sequence of events. Just knowing the possible dangers of such action could cause, especially at the hour that the incident was to occur, would it not make sense to have body cameras to ensure that the situation was handled properly?

It is a downright shame that we cannot trust the police to provide the correct information. I have firsthand knowledge of how police handle similar situations. In 1979, a friend and I were in my car, sitting and talking at the lakefront in Chicago, Illinois. It was approximately 2:00 a.m. We had left a nightclub and just decided to stop at the lakefront on a summer night and chill for a while.

At that time, I did not know that people could not visit the lakefront when the area was considered closed. I was in a brand-new 1979 Cadillac Eldorado. The car belonged to me, a young, twenty-four-year-old Black man. During that time, the Cadillac Eldorado was a car that was primarily driven by drug dealers, pimps, and gang leaders (I was none of those).

While sitting there, a car drove up. The car's lights were off, and it was unmarked. When the car approached my vehicle, two men jumped out with guns drawn, stating, "Get out of the car." They had no police uniforms on, no name tags, and were in an unmarked car. While being held at gunpoint, one of the police officers searched us as well as the car. Only after searching my car did they identify themselves as police officers.

I am well aware that the police have the right to stop and search a vehicle at any time. However, they must identify themselves as police officers. I had absolutely no idea that they were police officers, and if I had a weapon, I would have used it out of fear for my life.

I used this incident to show that I know firsthand what police are capable of doing. If I had not experienced the incident myself, I would never have believed that anything like this could happen. I really believe that the plainclothes officers just knew they were going to be able to arrest the two young Black men that day. I am sure that they were surprised to see there were no drugs and that I was employed as a city of Chicago college instructor.

Thank God that I did not panic. This definitely could have been a deadly situation. To this day, I do not understand why the police officers did not identify themselves as police officers when they approached my vehicle.

Police and law enforcement officials have the legal right to take people's lives. With that power, they must be held to the highest level of accountability and public trust. *Such accountability and public trust do not exist today.*

AN OVERVIEW OF THE COURTS

Once a person is accused of a crime, the prosecutors decide based on the evidentiary record to go to trial. This can be a very tedious process. The defendant generally has an attorney. If not, the courts generally assign an attorney. Defendants can also opt to represent themselves.

It is always best for people not to represent themselves in any criminal court proceeding, although sometimes, the accused could be their best legal defense because they may know all the best questions to ask accusers or witnesses as well as how to best attack the so-called evidence that was presented against them. However, it is very difficult for people to try and defend themselves in a court of law for many reasons, including the following:

1. It is very difficult to maintain a calm and level temperament when defending yourself. Most of the time, the alleged criminal knows exactly who is lying and/or fabricating the truth. While cross-examining the witnesses, it is very difficult to keep your composure when people are telling one lie after the next. I can tell you from my own experience that this is a very difficult thing to do. You just want to shout out that you are lying and you know it. Law School 101: a lawyer should never defend himself in any criminal court proceeding. History has shown that there are very few legal self-defenders that have been successful in winning their own criminal cases.

2. Most judges frown on legal self-defenders. If the legal self-defender is not a lawyer, he will not be totally aware of the structured courtroom procedures and will lack the legalese knowledge that would make for a smooth courtroom flow. If the defendant is a lawyer, many judges will frown on his decision to self-defend as well, which may cause the judge to stick to stricter courtroom procedure, leading to a more stressed courtroom atmosphere. Judges know that lawyers know that self-defending is a no-no.

3. It is very difficult for all parties to keep a professional composure when cross-examination is being done by a defendant while attempting to self-defend.

Oftentimes, a defendant does not have the access to a good criminal attorney. Due to lack of financial resources, the defendant has to be represented by a public defender or a less competent attorney, which in many cases will cause a case to be settled for a lesser charge/sentence or the defendant being found guilty where the outcome would have been different with a better or more experienced attorney.

Public defenders are better than not having any defense attorney at all. However, they generally do not represent a defendant as well as an experienced private attorney would—basically because a private attorney gets paid based on his experience and reputation (success rate). The better criminal defense attorneys are expensive. They tend to be well worth the extra money because they tend to get the best results. One thing for sure, the better the attorney, the better chances for a more favorable outcome to the defendant.

Many public defenders are quick to try and get the defendant to accept a plea deal. This is where the defendant pleads guilty or no contest to a charge in exchange for a reduced sentence. Sometimes, the public defender will try to get the defendant to agree to a lesser crime or charge (e.g., to reduce a charge from a felony to a misdemeanor).

Public defenders often have very large workloads and do not always have the defendant's best interest in mind. Therefore, public defenders push hard to try and close a case. Even when a public defender knows that a case has merit, he may still attempt to have the defendant take the easy way out, primarily because the public defender knows that he has less time and resources to devote to a full trial.

I feel that many defendants accept plea bargain deals when they probably should not. However, it is not always a bad thing. If you are assigned a public defender that is not going to devote the time that is needed in a case, it is better to accept the settlement than to risk losing a case and getting convicted of a higher level crime and facing a greater sentence or more aggressive fines.

Depending on the nature of the crime, you are most likely better being defended by a private attorney specializing in criminal trial defense. When prosecutors have high-profile cases, they generally pull out their top attorneys to handle these cases. Prosecutors generally have far greater resources to draw from in preparing their case and hearing. This means that they can hire expert witnesses, have animation presentations, as well as many other things that cost a lot of money. The more experienced private defense attorneys are generally far more equipped to offset this process with their own animation presentations or expert witnesses.

The bottom line is that you generally get what you pay for. There is no guarantee on the more money one spends, the more they would be successful. However, it sure does improve their odds of being successful.

Keep in mind that a good experienced private defense attorney is capable of doing everything that a prosecutor can do and more. *Is there any wonder why the rich have less convictions?*

Every now and then, a defendant gets lucky, and a lawyer or law firm will take a case pro bono (free of charge). This frequently happens in high-profile or heavily publicized cases. There is generally an ulterior motive for lawyers in taking such cases. The following are some of the reasons that lawyers take cases on a pro bono basis:

1. The case is considered a high-profile case. Many lawyers or law firms will take these cases with no fees to the defendant. Winning a high-profile case can prove to be invaluable to a lawyer or law firm. It can take a no-name lawyer or law

firm right to the forefront of success, which, in turn, would bring in significant future revenues and recognition. Many lawyers and law firms are aware of this and are willing to take on the risk for notoriety, fame, and/or future profits.

2. Some lawyers and law firms seek out various cases in which they feel that the defendant was treated unjustly. The main purpose of these lawyers and/or law firms is to bring justice to a defendant whom they feel was treated unjustly by the legal system.

3. Some lawyers and law firms will seek out cases that they have a strong opinion about, or issues involved in the case or involving a matter is something that they have an interest in. Oftentimes, lawyers and law firms will take on cases without monetary charges to support an interest or belief that they share.

After a lawyer has been chosen by a defendant, it is time to get ready for trial. The defendant has a choice to have a trial by jury or to have a judge solely make the determination of innocence or guilt. There can be pros and cons to both.

Before I review the trial process, I have to explain the plea bargain process. A plea deal can be brought up by the prosecuting attorney or the defendant's attorney. So what is a plea bargain? A plea bargain is where a prosecuting attorney and a defendant's attorney agree on a set of terms or conditions to settle a court case generally done prior to a court proceeding but can also be agreed upon during the course of the trial or at the end of a trial before the judge of jury render a verdict.

Generally, plea bargains save money by reducing court/trial time and attorney costs for the prosecutor as well as the defendant. On somewhat minor criminal offenses, it is common to interject a plea bargain to get the case settled in an expeditious, cost-effective manner. Generally, the original charge is reduced to a lesser charge. The defendant is granted less or no jail time than he would have received if found guilty of the original charge. Oftentimes, some type of probationary period may be offered as well.

The problem with plea bargains are that many are not really in the best interest of the defendant. Plea bargains can be good when defendants are really guilty of a criminal offense, and the defendants can get a break, especially if they are a first-time offender. Generally, a defendant's lawyer will advise defendant on the benefits of the plea bargain. Plea bargains can work well if administered fairly and equitably.

On the other hand, a plea bargain can be a bad choice and have devastating effects. This is when the plea deal being presented is not fair and equitable. Many times, defendants are offered a plea bargain when they are totally innocent of the crime that they allegedly committed. The sad part is that many innocent defendants will accept the plea bargain to avoid the possibility of being found guilty of a crime and being sentenced to a lengthy jail time.

Unfortunately, even if a person is innocent of a crime, they generally have a fifty-fifty chance of success. This is especially true when it comes to Black and Brown people, so it is generally easier for a Black or Brown person to accept a plea bargain. Most of the time Black and Brown people lack the finances or support systems that are necessary for good legal representation.

Plea bargains can come at a cost down the road. If a person was charged with a felony offense and it was plea-bargained down to a misdemeanor, the original charge is still a felony. When filling out job applications, a person that was charged with a felony must list that charge on the application regardless of its reduction to a lesser misdemeanor crime. Therefore, if an application asks an applicant if he has ever been charged with a felony offense, the applicant must answer yes to this question.

I find that many people who accept a plea bargain don't understand that they were still charged with a felony offense but being convicted of a lesser offense. This can become a problem as some employers will not consider people for employment with a previous felony charge regardless of the conviction.

Moreover, many people don't know how to correctly answer the question because they think that the felony charge goes away after they have accepted the plea agreement of a lesser charge. The correct way to answer the question, "Have you ever been charged with a felony offense?" is to state yes. Then in the comments section, you are to list that the felony offense was reduced to a misdemeanor. Failure to correctly answer this question has cost many people jobs that they would have obtained had they answered the question correctly. Many people are just not aware that when charged with a felony offense that charge is part of the original arrest file and court records.

Note: the same is true for any criminal charges. If a person is charged with a crime, they must list the charge on any employment or background investigation even if the charge was dismissed or reduced. Therefore, even if you are found innocent of a crime and the charges were dismissed, you still must list that you were charged with the criminal offense. The only exception is if the record was expunged, which means it will be stricken from all court records and files.

Even with the court records being expunged, the police department will have a record of the arrest and the alleged charge, which means that people must be extremely careful in how they answer these questions on applications. Therefore, if an application asks if you have ever been arrested, you must answer yes even if the charges were dismissed in court and the record was expunged.

It is so unfortunate that so many people are not aware of this. A store manager brought this matter to my attention. We were talking, and he brought up the fact that he could not understand why so many of his minority applicants could not pass their background investigations for employment. He stated that at least 90 percent of the African American males would fail the background investigation based on the information that they had supplied on their employment applications.

I asked him to try this: in the next employment recruitment seminar, tell all applicants to make sure that they list any previous arrests, charges, or convictions on employment application and to explain the circumstances to include final disposition in the comments.

To his surprise, 90 percent of the African American applicants were now passing the employment background investigations. To my surprise, even the store manager did not understand how the people were passing the background investigation after listing previous arrest records.

I was finally able to get the store manager to understand that the misdemeanor arrest records were not the cause for African Americans' not passing the background investigations. But instead, the primary reason was falsification on the application. Meaning, that the applicants failed to list all information correctly as required.

My personal feelings on plea bargains are as follows: they can be good and bad. The good part is that if a person committed a minor offense, he could possibly avoid jail time and get the matter settled much quicker. Sometimes, the charge can be reduced from a felony to a misdemeanor. This can work out very well, especially if the person accepting the plea bargain is guilty of the crime as charged.

The bad part is if the person is not guilty of the crime as charged. Many people are encouraged to accept a plea bargain even when they are completely innocent of the crime as charged. Unfortunately, sometimes it is better to plead guilty to a lesser crime and get probation than to go through a trial in which the defendant could be found guilty. If found guilty, the defendant may have to face jail time in addition to being convicted of a more serious offense.

If a defendant is found guilty by a court trial, there are no more settlement offers. The defendant has to accept the sentence as well as the terms for jail time, fines, etc. The defendant does have the option to appeal the guilty verdict if for some reason he feels that the first trial was unjust.

Just because the defendant requests an appeal does not mean that the appellant court will grant an appeal. All appeal requests are reviewed by the appellant judges, and they decide if the request validates an appeal hearing. Approximately one-third of the cases that request an appeal is granted an appeal hearing. Even more disturbing is that out of the one-third that gets a hearing, approximately one-third of the cases that are heard will get overturned, which means that there is a greater possibility that a case heard on appeal will not be overturned.

Given those odds, sometimes it is better to take the plea deal. I know that it does not seem fair. That is why it is very important for a defendant's attorney to advise the defendant of exactly what the attorney feels are the defendant's chances for a positive outcome of a trial. If the attorney is honest in his assessment of the situation, it will at least give the defendant a reasonable assessment of his chances of winning the case.

Keep in mind that there are no guarantees on winning a criminal case. One of the most interesting things about trials is that it could appear to be a 100 percent winning case at the start of a trial and one turn of events, could change the outcome of the case.

The same can be true in a case that is based on circumstantial evidence. It can appear that there is no way that the defendant would win the case. Then in a turn of events during the hearing, things change and bring about a different than expected outcome.

What many people don't realize is that trials can be very tricky. It does not matter if a person is innocent or guilty. In essence, with most trials, the defendant is rolling the dice. Of course, having a highly experienced attorney improves a defendant's chances for a more positive outcome.

It is very difficult for many people innocent of a crime to take a plea deal. However, sometimes, it can be their best alternative given the circumstances.

I personally became aware of this situation while undergoing a trial hearing in which I had failed to agree with charges filed against me by a federal agency in which I was terminated by the agency. To my surprise, at the end of the trial hearing (prior to receiving the judge's decision), the judge asked me if I would be willing to accept a settlement offer. Before I could even respond, the judge had the agency's attorney present a proposed settlement offer. The offer included the following terms and conditions that I would have to agree to:

- Return to work as a time-served suspension
- Accept a lesser position and pay grade demotion
- Be reassigned to a position of the agency's choosing

I declined to accept the agency's settlement offer primarily for the following reasons:

- I was 100 percent innocent of the charges filed against me.
- I had already been out of work for over a year (any damages from being unemployed had already occurred).
- Last but not least, I expressed to the judge that I could not understand why the agency would make an offer to return me to employment with criminal charges that even if were true, no one in their right mind would offer a person reemployment as one of the charges was deception of federal funds.

My response to the judge was *if I am guilty as charged and committed the acts that I am accused of for the reasons that I am accused of, then I deserved to be fired.*

The judge told me to think about the offer and that I could accept the offer any time prior to his written decision on the case. He said it would be approximately forty-five to sixty days for his finale written decision.

Well, it took ninety days to get his written decision. Many times during that ninety-day period, I did rethink that maybe I did make a mistake. I could have been back at work and at least getting a paycheck.

After conferring with my attorney, she told me that she was 100 percent sure that the federal agency did not prove their case against me. She further explained that if the judge did not rule in our favor, it could take another six to nine months to get an appeal decision. Therefore, she was letting me know that I still could be out of work for approximately another year. She went on to explain that most people facing a similar situation would agree to accept the settlement offer because they don't want to go another year without a paycheck.

Based on the hearing and evidence presented, my attorney and I were confident that the judge was going to overturn the removal. But to our surprise, the judge upheld the agency's removal. This was really disturbing in that the testimony at trial clearly proved that both charges filed against me had no merit whatsoever. In fact, one of the charged acts of wrongdoing was still being done by the current management. Not only was the practice still being done, it was corroborated through testimony that the same procedures were in place and implemented prior to my managing the operation.

We appealed the decision. The appeal process took about approximately nine months. The removal was overturned on appeal. What was so surprising in this case was that even the appeal judges could not understand how the initial judge could come to a guilty verdict given the transcript of the trial. The appeal judges even asked the initial trial judge to explain how he reached his guilty finding. His response to the appeal judges was that the defendant's testimony lacked credibility. He further stated that he found all testimony presented against the defendant had greater credibility.

The appeal judges found the initial judge's response interesting, so interesting that they requested that the trial transcripts be sent to them. They wanted to hear exactly what he heard that contributed to his guilty finding. The initial judge responded to the appeal judges that the audio transcript of the trial had mistakenly got destroyed. I guess that I can consider myself one of the lucky ones. As I learned in law school, every innocent person does not win their case.

This case is a clear example of how a judge can rule against an individual based on other reasons. This was clearly a prima facie case of innocence, yet I was found guilty. To this day, I cannot understand why? Was it racism? If it was not, then what else could it have been?

I know that it is easy for people to say, "Great! You eventually won." Well, winning a year later on appeal for an employment removal that should not have occurred in the first place? The only reason that I was victorious in this case was that I was treated like dirt and was willing to endure the pain for a chance at real justice.

Keep in mind, if I had lost the case, I would have lost everything, including job, pension, and back pay. This is why the decision to give in or to push on can be very difficult.

There is even a bigger problem. After winning and returning to work, how do you go back and be a viable employee after a whole system lied and brought false charges against you? I sat through a trial and watched my bosses, federal law enforcement officials, and subordinate employees get on the stand and lie, lie, lie. How can you go back and trust a system that clearly demonstrated that they have no integrity?

Guess what; you can't (at least, I could not). So in summary, I still ended up losing my job (basically because I no longer had confidence in my employer). How can anyone survive in an environment that they can't trust their bosses, coworkers, subordinates, or the agency's law enforcement. Bottom line, I can forgive a misunderstanding or difference of opinion. However, it is impossible to forgive an outright lie.

Needless to say, this incident ultimately cost me my job. Lucky for me, I was able to mitigate the blow. After being off work for almost two years, I figured out that even if I won the case, there was no way that I would just go back to work and pretend that nothing ever happened. My primary reason for returning was to bring shame to the agency.

Through the federal management structure, my management position was protected, which means that if I was successful in overturning the agency's removal, I would have to be assigned back to my original position and duty station.

Well, losing the removal and returning to work with full back pay was very embarrassing for the agency, but having to place me back in my original position was even more hurtful. After the agency returned me to work, before returning to my original assigned location, I was asked to choose another office or work location. I was offered any similar position that was open even if it was a higher pay level and grade.

I refused. I insisted on being placed back in my original position. Management was totally upset with my decision as it made them look very bad. They had a removal overturned in which they could not get a reassignment or any other disciplinary action out of the incident.

Needless to say, the subsequent treatment that I received from management was horrendous. I stayed approximately five additional years until I had had enough. I left on an early retirement EEO settlement. As can be seen, I won a battle but not the war.

Criminal Cases

Once it is determined that a criminal case is going to trial, it is time for the defendant to pick the method of how the outcome will be determined. He has the option to choose a trial by jury or a bench trial (a bench trial is where the judge is the sole person making the decision). The judge alone will decide the defendant's innocence or guilt.

If a defendant chooses to have a jury trial, twelve people are selected to hear and decide the case based on the testimony and evidence as presented at trial. Most of the time, the general population is advised to choose the trial-by-jury option. The basic theory is that the more people you have making the decision, the better chances for a more fair outcome.

My thoughts on jury trials vs. bench trials: On its face, the jury trial would generally be the best way for a defendant to go. Generally, it is harder to get twelve people to come to the same conclusion. The problem that I have with the jury trial is that they are not always as fair as they appear.

We have to keep in mind that when the justice system was set up in America. Black people were not considered as equal citizens. It is hard to impossible to believe that Black people could have received blind justice accordingly. Unfortunately, this still holds true today. Many White people have no idea what Black people face in their everyday lives.

I had a White friend once tell me that he did not believe that Black people are being discriminated against in today's society. He felt that most Black people just play the race card whenever they get in trouble or when they feel that it could benefit them in some kind of way. I do have to agree that this indeed happens in some cases. However, I explained to him that his perception is not totally accurate as racism does exist overwhelmingly in the United States.

It is very difficult for White people to understand the life differences that Black people face in our society. To some, it may be hard to believe that one group of people are treated differently from another group. There are many things that Black and Brown people face daily that Whites have never faced or faced on a very limited basis, including some of the following:

Racial profiling, such as stopping and frisking Black people for no apparent reason. Almost every Black male in any major city has been a victim. As a young Black man, I was stopped constantly by the Chicago Police Department while driving my vehicle. While driving a Cadillac Eldorado, I was stopped at least once a week. I had the car for two years; within those two years, I was stopped at least once a week. The police would always have me step out of the car while they search the car.

What bothered me the most was that I was being stopped and searched for no apparent reason other than being a Black male. I can't even describe how it made me feel each time that I was stopped. When I would talk to my White coworkers and associates about the police harassment, they all thought that it was terrible and found it hard to believe, especially the frequency that it occurred. However, none of them had ever experienced that level of harassment, and most had never even been stopped by a police officer while driving unless it was for a traffic violation. I would explain to my White friends and associates that they would never understand the feeling unless they had experienced the incidents firsthand.

As terrible as they thought it was, the actual experience was ten times worse (as a victim). At the time, I was a college graduate and was working two jobs. To add insult to injury, one of my jobs was as a teacher for the city of Chicago. Yes, I was employed with the city of Chicago, which was the same employer as the Chicago police officers that were stopping and searching my vehicle. No person should ever have to face anything like this. However, it was a common occurrence in the 1970s, and it still exists today.

Many times, Black people are denied promotions or employment opportunities just because of their race. It was worse during the twentieth century, but it still exists today. As a Black man, I have been a victim of employment discrimination. I have been denied employment opportunities and promotions due to racism.

How does one know he's being discriminated against? When one applicant has far superior qualifications than the person that was selected for the position. Can you believe that I was once denied a one-pay-grade-level promotion in a position that I had already held at a one-pay-grade-lower level. The person recommended for the position was in a three-pay-grade-lower level than the posted position. He was a White male. He had high school diploma with approximately eight years of management experience. I had a master of public administration degree and over twenty years of management experience. I was already in a similar lower grade level position and was fully qualified for the posted position. Not only was I highly qualified for the posted position; I was also the most qualified of the other applicants.

To add more insult, there had been no Black males or Black females promoted to the grade level position that I applied for in the North Suburban Region since the restructure and current management that had been in place since 1992 (the incident occurred in 2001). There were over twenty such positions in the Northern Illinois district.

Racial discrimination is real, and it hurts to see a White male with half your qualifications get promoted over you. Not only did it happen to me, I have seen it happen time and time again to other Blacks, women, and other minorities. Those are just a few of the racial disparities that Black people still face on a daily basis. There are so many more.

Let's take a critical look at our jury system. A jury is supposed to be made up based on a defendant's peers. For the most part, it is next to impossible for an all-White jury to fairly evaluate criminal charges against a Black person because of the lack of understanding between the races. Whites don't fully have a sense of exactly what Black people face.

To be honest, I did not think that a law enforcement agency would lie on people and/or misrepresent facts to make someone guilty, especially when all evidence clearly shows no guilt. Unfortunately, I found out the hard way that this is not the case. I was previously a federal employee and in charge of a very large financial operation. There were a few government investigators that were auditing my operation. We had different views of how the operation should be managed. Their views were based on their opinions, and my views were based on financial operation books as well as prior management experience.

Needless to say, the investigation then turned into a witch hunt. The investigators started running my operation, directing my employees' duties, and holding me responsible and accountable for the investigator's actions. One investigator told me, "I am going to get your Black ass," and another investigator told me, "I am going to build and make a case against you." Well, that is exactly what they did. The investigative agency built a case against me. The problem with the investigative case was that it was filled with lies and misrepresentations.

I was totally shocked when I saw the charges being placed against me were all based on a fraudulent investigative report. To this day, I cannot see or understand how sworn law enforcement officers could do this as well as get away with it.

The case was filled with false statements. My superiors used the investigative report against me, and I was fired based on the investigative report's listed findings. These were the subsequent events:

- I was given a date by my superiors to discuss the charges. In the letter, it clearly stated that I was entitled to have representation of my choosing at the assigned meeting.
- I responded that I would be attending the meeting and would be represented by an attorney.
- I was sent a letter notifying me that the meeting was canceled, discharging me of my duties, and proposing that I be removed from my position as well as from US Government service.
- The charges and removal were eventually overturned on appeal, and I was reinstated to the position that I held prior to removal.

The entire removal process was a sham. If this had not happened to me, I would have never believed that something like this could happen.

One thing for sure, the whole process taught me that an employer can mess your whole life up even by making false allegations because you have to be able to ride out the storm. Fortunately, I was single and did not have a family that was dependent on my income. For that reason, I was willing to risk everything to prove my innocence.

It was the most difficult challenge that I ever faced. At the time, I have over twenty years of management experience, so one would think that it would be easy to go out and find another job. Well, it is just not that easy. Try to get a job making a hundred thousand dollars a year with no references. Although I had the experience, I had no references. Then when asked, "Why did you leave your previous employer?" I would have to disclose that I was fired. Next, I would have to explain the circumstances, which I was basically charged with misappropriation of funds. Try to tell a potential employer that and see where it gets you.

Moreover, see the reaction when you tell the interviewer that the whole removal from your position was a sham and the charges are all false, and watch the expression of the interviewer's face as they tell you to come back when or if you get the situation rectified. The bottom line is that I was strapped. I quickly realized that I was not going to get reemployed making anywhere close to the money that I was previously making.

In US Government employment, when a person is involuntarily terminated, they remain on the rolls while exhausting their grievance and appeal rights. Because I was still considered an employee in a nonwork-nonpay status, I was not able to withdraw my 401K plan. You can only withdraw funds from the 401K savings plan once you are removed from the rolls, which meant that the only way for me to obtain any money from the 401K program is that I had to drop my grievances and appeals. This was very stressful, especially realizing that I would not be able to obtain employment anywhere close to what I was making prior to the involuntary termination. After applying for several positions, it became apparent that the only jobs that I was going to find were entry-level positions.

The real stress in this situation is that you don't know if you are going to win or lose. The other thing that I had to think about was my retirement. If the removal stuck, I would lose all my retirement benefits. At that time, I had approximately eighty thousand dollars that I had paid into the retirement program. If the termination were to stand, I would be able to collect all the funds that I paid into the retirement plan (approximately eighty thousand).

So I had a lot to think about while making my decision to fight the termination:

The hardest part of the decision was looking at over two hundred thousand dollars in 401K plan and CSI retirement plan, which is a lot of money when no money is coming in. However, I can see why so many people turn to drugs or depression. Thank goodness that I was young enough to start over when the incident occurred. I was hopeful that I would win my job back. But I was also realistic; there was a real possibility that I would lose that battle.

With that in mind, I decided that I would pursue a law degree. I felt that if I lost my case against the US Government, it would be an easier path to return to the financial income status that I was used to having before my termination. Well, fortunately for me, I was reinstated to my position. I continued working on a law degree part-time. I am so happy that I decided to get the law degree. In the long run, it turned out to be a lifesaver.

Even though I won the case, my career with the agency was shot. First of all, how can a person go back and be a viable employee when he can't trust the people that he is working for or working with? I tried. I just could not do it. I ended up leaving the agency after twenty-five years of service.

Although I still ended up paying a hefty price by giving up my job, I did not leave empty-handed. I was granted a payout. It was a good enough offer for me to accept. Trust me, this would have not happened had I not been well versed in the law. I did not go to law school for nothing, I had a few tricks up my sleeve when I returned to government employment, and everything worked out perfectly, just as predicted.

The thing that I found most interesting about the whole ordeal was most of my fellow coworkers, peers, subordinates, and superiors actually believed that I was really guilty of something that led to my previous termination. They felt that I had a good attorney who was able to get me off the hook. Most people were under the impression that I won my case because of a technicality. Many of my Black coworkers were fully aware that similar attacks on Black employees were common, and many had been victims themselves or at least had observed similar incidences.

I am of the firm belief that only Black and Brown people can fully understand what other Blacks and Brown people go through in their lives and surroundings. It is very difficult to understand or believe what you have never experienced or witnessed. I really believe the reason that I was successful in my termination proceedings was that I witnessed similar incidents all the time. I was well aware of the organization's disparate treatment of Black and Brown people. As a matter of fact, I had gotten to the point that I was looking forward to the challenge as I knew that my turn was coming.

Based on my background, life, and experience, I strongly feel that for a jury to be most fair to a Black, Brown, or other minority, it must consist of at least three-fourths of the minority that is being accused. Moreover, at least three-fourths of the jury should also include the same gender to the greatest extent possible.

The reason why gender is so important is that although most people are aware that minorities are treated differently, Black and Brown men face different obstacles than Black and Brown women. For example, most Black or Brown women have no knowledge as to how it feels to be stopped and frisked for no reason. It is ironic because I know women that have illegally carried guns their entire adult lives and have never been searched. If it had been me (a Black man), I would have had over one hundred charges of illegal possession of a handgun. The same would be true for any other Black or Brown man. There are very few Black and Brown men that have not been stopped and searched in the inner cities.

Therefore, I have come to the conclusion that for a jury to be fair to Black and Brown people, the jury needs to know exactly what it is like to walk in the same shoes. It just makes for a level playing field, something that most Black and Brown people have never had. Most White people just don't fully understand the obstacles that

Black and Brown people face within their neighborhoods, families, and work lives. One thing for sure, Black and Brown living experiences are totally different from most White people.

Don't get me wrong, the jury (no matter what the makeup) sometimes can get it right. But many times, they don't. The primary cause has to be a lack of understanding of Black and minority lifestyles, environments, and experiences. After all, Blacks and other minorities should be entitled to the same justice system as Whites. Equal justice can never happen under the current justice system.

Unfortunately, the American court system is yet another victim of systemic racism. Our court system was never designed to be fair to all people, and to this very day, it does not fairly serve Black, Brown, and other minority people. Historically, most White alleged criminals have had a majority-White jury. Most people are aware that an all-White jury will produce different results than an all-Black jury. Gee, I wonder why? This is ridiculous considering that the United States Justice System always insisted that justice is blind. We all know that is a lie.

This is something that I have not only seen but have felt and experienced. Historically, the American judicial system has underserved Black, Brown, and other minorities. The current system just does not work as well for Black, Brown, and minorities as it does for White Americans, and it never has.

Because America has a huge problem with systemic racism, it just cannot get it right when it comes down to judging and treating Black and Brown people fairly. One thing for sure, our jury selection system is not as fair as it should be to any and all races and backgrounds; it has to be overhauled. In an ideal world, it would work perfectly. However, America is not ideal. There is a serious racial issue in this country.

Any rational person knows that a criminal justice system is only as good as the people that make up the system. When you have a criminal justice system that is filled with racist judges, juries, prosecutors, and law enforcement officers, it is impossible to have blind justice.

Trials

Then comes the trial and courtroom hearing. Trials can be interesting because you never know what twists and turns may occur during the course of the hearing. Some trials, before they occur, may appear as a 100 percent win but ends up being a loser. And some trials can appear to be a 100 percent loser prior to the hearing and end up a winner.

Criminal trial outcomes are largely dependent upon witness testimony. Lawyers on both sides generally work very hard to try to discredit the other side's witnesses. I like to consider most trials as an artist drawing competition. The artist (lawyer) that paints the best picture wins, which equates to the lawyer that makes the most convincing argument to a jury or judge generally wins the case.

The defendant may or may not testify. Generally, that decision is made on the recommendation of the defendant's attorney. In some cases, it is beneficial for the defendant to testify, and in some cases, it is not. There is no right or wrong answer here. Most often, a defendant's testimony can make or break a case.

Oftentimes, the defendant's attorney does not make the final decision for a defendant to testify until close to the end of a trial. The attorney weighs the scope of how he feels the trial is going. If he feels that it is not looking good for the defendant, he may feel that it is in the defendant's best interest to testify. Sometimes, if things are not looking good for the defendant, his attorney may have the defendant testify as a last-ditch effort—something like what do we have to lose? Sometimes it works in the defendant's favor and sometimes not.

There are many factors that can go into the decision for a defendant to testify in his own trial:

- How well the defendant may appear to a jury. Some defendants just look more guilty than others. Some have a strong appearance, and some have a weak appearance. Depending on the case, self-testimony can be an advantage or disadvantage.

- Some people come across very well on the stand, and some don't. Many times, the defendant's attorney can make that determination based on his ongoing communication with the defendant.
- If the defendant is not sharp, he can get tripped up on cross-examination by the prosecuting attorneys. Many prosecuting attorneys are pros at what they do and can rattle even the strongest of people.
- Cross-examination can be very tricky, and many defendants will have a hard time keeping composure while being questioned. Keep in mind, the prosecutor is not the defendant's friend. The prosecutor is out to win. If the defendant is unable to handle the harsh, stringent questioning of a prosecutor, it may be to his advantage not to testify.
- One thing for sure, lawyers generally have a good idea of who would be best at testifying in their own defense. I would strongly recommend that defendants take the advice of their attorney. Many cases are won or lost based on the defendant's testimony.

The biggest thing that most people are not prepared for during a trial is the lies that are going to be told by the witnesses during the trial. Many witnesses, especially the ones testifying against the defendant, will lie or at least be less than truthful. It is almost as if they are encouraged to lie. The prosecution will oftentimes tell their witnesses exactly what they want them to say. It generally appears next to impossible to get the entire truth during a criminal trial from either the defendant or the witnesses testifying against or for him.

For some reason, many defendants will lie to their lawyer. I really can't understand why. It is always in the best interests to tell the lawyer the truth and let the lawyer figure out how to defend the case from there. It appears that many defendants don't want to look bad to their attorney or that they just want their story to be believed by their attorney. Whatever the reason, it is not good. Many cases are lost because the defendant did not fully disclose information or provided less than truthful information to their attorney.

What many people don't understand is that an attorney builds his case on the information that is provided to them. When the attorney is gathering information from the defendant, he needs clear-cut answers. The defendant should be truthful with all information that he provides to his attorney. This is very instrumental when the defendant's attorney cross-examine witnesses' testimony. If the attorney is confident that his client has been totally truthful, he can best defend and structure his arguments.

The big problem with defendants lying is that the court generally holds them to a higher standard. If the defendant is caught in a lie, he will most likely lose his case. As they say, credibility means everything. However, it only appears to be applicable to the defendant. It does not matter whether the defendant is guilty or not; if he or his attorney is caught lying or providing untrue information to the court, he most likely will be found guilty.

The best advice that I can give a defendant is to always tell your attorney the truth. Some attorneys will ask their client if they are guilty of the alleged crime, and they expect a truthful answer. Admitting guilt to their attorney does not mean that the attorney will work any less than if the defendant was innocent of the crime. Sometimes, a defendant could be guilty of a crime and still be found innocent of the charges in court. Sometimes, even though a defendant is found guilty, his sentence could be reduced based on mitigating circumstances. A defendant's attorney's job is to provide the best defense possible for his client, which means the defendant's attorney will not always win a case, but many times he can definitely get the best sentence possible when the defendant is found guilty.

On the other hand, one of the most disturbing parts of a trial is when the witnesses get up and tell one lie after another.

It is very difficult for any defendant to keep his composure when people take the witness stand under oath and just flat out lie. Most defendant's attorneys will try to prepare their clients ahead of time to expect the prosecution witnesses to lie. However, this is a very difficult task to endure. This will oftentimes cause a defendant to cry, become verbally expressive, or show some type of emotion during the testimony. Defendants have to be very careful in expressing emotion during a trial. Sometimes, it can work in their favor and sometimes not. Keep in mind, generally, a jury is watching, and they observe the defendant's emotions. Loud outbursts and making noises can cause disruption in the court, which can result in the defendant being fined or removed from the hearing.

Many attorneys would agree that an ability of a defendant to control emotions or to know how to display certain emotions can be pivotal in jury decisions. For example, a defendant crying when a witness makes certain comments can cause jurors to also become emotional, or a defendant showing an expression of surprise by certain comments made by witnesses could cause jurors to doubt the testimony being given. Firsthand knowledge helped me fully understand the gravity of this matter.

During a Merit Systems Protection Board hearing in which I was the defendant, the hardest thing for me to endure was watching the agency witnesses take the stand and tell one lie after the next. I just wanted to shout out, "You are telling a damn lie!"

The agency investigators took the witness stand and provided evidence that was false to include statements and situations that they created in an effort to substantiate my removal. Moreover, they were able to get several witnesses to lie and corroborate with them. Through testimony and factual documentation, all alleged charges were proven to be false, which meant, that the agency witnesses lied and committed fraud. However, no one was held in contempt. They were able to just lie and have no accountability for their actions.

Even more disturbing, how does a person, after winning such a case, go back to work with superiors, coworkers, subordinates, and agency investigators who all lied and conspired against you? The answer is that it is very difficult, and many will not survive the pressure and aftermath that they will face upon return. For me personally, law school may have been a lifesaver.

This is totally unfair to a defendant because if the defendant is caught lying, he will most likely lose his case. If the prosecution lies, nothing happens. The prosecution in this case lost. Moreover, they presented many acts of perjury while presenting their case, and someone should have faced criminal charges. Until the court systems really start taking perjury seriously, there will always be a problem with fair justice for all.

In this case, the bare minimum that all people caught lying should have faced was removal from government employment. These government officials created a terrible situation that made for a toxic work environment once I returned. No matter how hard that I tried, and I did try hard, I could not forget the level of treatment that I received during the whole termination process. I just could not understand how a decent person/employee could have been treated the way that I was. I no longer had trust or faith in the system and had no choice but to eventually leave. Therefore, everything that I fought for, I ended up losing anyway.

As can be seen, lies can have devastating effects on people's lives, employment, and family while the prosecution gets away scot-free. Even though I returned to work, the big question is did I really win? The answer is no. In the end, I still came out the loser.

All people should be held accountable for perjury. It is the law, and it is rarely followed. Our justice system will definitely be much fairer to all people if everyone is held accountable for perjury. Anyone and everyone caught intentionally lying should and must be penalized for the system to be fair for all.

Once the trial is over, the defendant will either be found innocent or guilty. If found guilty, most of the jail time (if any) generally starts immediately after the trial. If found innocent, the defendant is generally free to leave and return to his regular life and surroundings.

Summary

I have come to the conclusion that the entire United States democracy is based on lies, starting with the US Constitution, which clearly states that "all men are created equal." If indeed this is the case, then why are Black and Brown people treated so differently? One can only come to the conclusion that America's whole design was set up for the sole benefit of the White race.

As I think about it now, what a disgrace it was to have to say the Pledge of Allegiance every day in grammar school:

> I pledge allegiance to the flag of the United States of America, and to the Republic for which it stands, one Nation under God, indivisible, with liberty and justice for all.

At that time, I really believed that there was liberty and justice for all. Life and living clearly taught me that this was simply not true.

In America I have learned that we say one thing and mean another, such as…

Innocent until proven guilty.

Anybody who has had any involvement with our criminal justice system knows that this is far from the truth. Based on my experiences, I would say that it would be more correct to say that you are guilty until proven innocent. *America has got to learn how to say what it means and to mean what it says.* This has to be done first and foremost before any other restructure can effectively take place.

The following are the recommendations that I see as necessary to finally get our justice system on the right track to ensure that there is liberty and equal justice for all:

Police Departments

It starts with the police departments. The current law enforcement system is so corrupt that it is ridiculous to think that a training class will correct the ingrained issues and problems that are deeply embedded in the system. The only way to fully correct our criminal justice system is to start over again.

I know that it sounds difficult, but it is not impossible, and it is totally necessary to correct a broken system. To better understand, let's take a close look at our current law enforcement policing structure.

Many police departments only require that a person pass an exam. Then they are placed on a roster, interviewed, hired, and trained. This may work in a society where all people are truly looked at and treated the same. However, it does not work in the United States.

Think about it. Police officers have the least requirement of any other profession that has control over life or death. Until recently, most police departments did not require a college degree. There are still many policing agencies that do not require a bachelor's degree. Some require an associate's degree, some just require some college (generally at least thirty or more college semester credit hours), and some just require a high school diploma. Keep in mind that once a police officer is hired, he is granted the highest possible authority. At his sole discretion, he decides who will live or die. Now that is a lot of power to grant to a single individual.

Granted, police officers have to justify their actions when a life has been taken. However, it is not as easy today to get away with police wrongdoing as it was in the past. Modern technology such as cell phones, videos, and cameras have made a big difference in bringing police officer's wrongdoings to light. Based on recent trends, we see that there is still a lot of wrongdoing police officers.

The only way that the United States can have a truly fair and just police department is that all police officers have to be held accountable for their actions. From day one, police have to be taught that all lives matter and that their job is to serve and protect all people. Moreover, they have to be taught to understand that a person is not guilty of a crime until he has been convicted of that crime, which means that simply charging a person with a crime does not mean that the person is guilty as charged. Furthermore, this means that a person is innocent until proven guilty and has been convicted of the crime as charged.

There is no secret to anyone that has any knowledge of policing that police officers have one of the strictest code-of-silence policies around. There is a long tradition of police supporting other police officer's wrongdoings, including committing wrongful deaths and human rights violations.

Those current practices and policies are so ingrained in the police structure that it is very difficult for a decent police officer to survive within the agency with integrity. How in the world do law enforcement agencies expect the general public to say something when they see something when the general public can't expect the police to do the same thing in return.

It has to be a grave injustice for most of the good police officers to watch the bad ones lie and commit numerous policy violations then get promoted while the good ones get nothing. Within the current law enforcement structure, the bad officers generally get the best rewards.

Because the current police internal structure is so corrupt, it has to be dismantled and restructured from the bottom up. Real change has to begin with the police. Once the general public sees that the police are totally respecting their rights as people, it will automatically change the current levels of distrust that the Black and Brown communities currently have.

Right now, there are really bad relations between many policing jurisdictions and minorities, especially Black people. All too frequently, Black people are being killed by police officers unjustly. It is hard to believe in today's society that police officers are killing people with absolutely no justification even while people are videotaping, taking pictures, and/or recording the transaction, as illustrated by a few of the following incidences:

In May 2020, a Black man, George Floyd, was killed by a Minneapolis, Minnesota, police offer. While attempting to arrest a Black man, three Minneapolis police officers held down a Black man that was handcuffed and accused of resisting arrest. Floyd was on the ground with one officer pressing his knee against Floyd's neck. One officer was at Floyd's midsection and one at his knees. One other officer was standing guard and was being used to control the gathering crowd.

Floyd started having a problem breathing and told the officers that he could not breathe. People started to gather around, and some started filming the incident. People started requesting the officer who had his knee on Floyd's neck to take it off his neck because Floyd appeared to be having breathing difficulties. Many of the bystanders began to become concerned about Floyd's pleas for help and his begging for the officer to remove his knee from Floyd's neck.

Out of concern, the crowd began speaking out. They asked the officer to remove his knee from Floyd's neck. They shouted to the officer many times that the officer was killing Floyd. They even asked the other officers to help Floyd. After approximately six minutes, Floyd stopped moving. The officer still kept his knee on Floyd's neck for an additional two minutes (approximately) even though Floyd became lifeless and was no longer moving or talking. When the paramedics arrived, Floyd had no pulse. He was taken away by ambulance and later pronounced dead.

It was clear and evident that Floyd was murdered at the scene by the police officer pressing his knee and body weight against Floyd's neck. The four officers that were involved were fired the very next day by the Minneapolis Police Department. However, none of the police officers were arrested and charged with murder until people started rioting in the streets some four days later. Even then, only one police officer was arrested and charged with third-degree murder—manslaughter, which is the lowest possible charge one can get for a nonaccidental murder.

It took approximately seven days of protesting and rioting for the other three officers to be arrested and charged with murder. Also around this time, they upgraded the murder charge against the first officer charged to second-degree murder, which I feel was the correct charge in this case.

The police officer that was charged with the actual murder of Floyd was White. At the time of writing this narrative, I am not sure of the races of the other three men, but from my observation, it appears that one was Asian, one was White, and one was mixed race (Black and some other race).

The question here is why did it take so long to make an arrest and bring charges against the other involved police officers? It was clear in all observed videos of this incident that all involved officers worked as a team during this incident. At any time during the incident, anyone of the assisting officers could have interjected and defused the situation leading to Floyd's death. Instead, they did absolutely nothing.

Let's go one step further. If this had been an incident involving non-police officers and the general public saw that four men were killing a man, after a couple of warnings from the crowd, it would have been acceptable for the crowd to take action up to using deadly force to stop the situation.

As I watch the videos of the incident, I often wonder if I had been licensed to carry a weapon and was at the scene, would I have shot the police officers involved? Which means that I would most likely be dead now. However, Mr. Floyd would most likely still be alive, and all the surviving police officers would still have a job. There most likely would have been no court hearing, and I would have been labeled a criminal. If I were to have lived after shooting the police officers, I definitely would be serving life in prison.

The bottom line is that no one could have helped Mr. Floyd without sacrificing their own lives. It is hard to watch a man die before your very eyes for no justifiable reason. It is so sad that something that seems relatively minor could escalate to something like this.

Moreover, I could not see how or why the situation escalated to this. I worked as a cashier in a grocery store for many years. The policy was that the cashier was responsible for making sure that all bills over ten dollars were checked and any that were questionable be rejected.

The news media stated that the store clerk took the twenty-dollar bill and gave Mr. Floyd the merchandise. Then after Mr. Floyd left the store, the clerk called the police, who, in turn, attempted to address the matter with Mr. Floyd outside the store.

During a television interview, the store manager stated that the clerk did not follow store policy. He stated that the forged twenty-dollar bill should have been caught at time of the purchase and not after the purchase was made. It was not the policy of the store to call the police for a single counterfeit bill.

Based on everything that I have seen and heard on media, I can see no reason why Mr. Floyd was being arrested in the first place. An incident report appears to have been the only necessary course of action for this incident.

I am of the opinion that all law enforcement officers need to be retrained. They need to fully understand their duties and respect the rights of all the people that they serve. We all know, though, that just because a person is accused of something does not mean that they are guilty. Right now, the culture is guilty until proven innocent, especially when it comes to Blacks and minorities.

If there is one good thing that came from this whole ordeal, it is that White and Black people came together in almost equal numbers to protest this unjust killing of a Black man. Hopefully, this is an indicator that all people are getting tired of the disparate treatment of Black and Brown people. Most importantly, they are not going to continue to tolerate it.

Many people are doubtful that law enforcement can or will change; I am not one of them. Law enforcement officials have to start being held accountable for their actions. Accountability will bring a change. This means that law enforcement officials have to stand up against other law enforcement officials when required to do so.

So you think that the above incident is not necessarily disparate or racial injustice? Well, let's take a look at another case that also involved the Minnesota Police Department. In July 2017, a Black Minneapolis police officer shot and killed a White woman while investigating a crime in progress call. News media reported that the White woman, a Minneapolis, Minnesota, resident, ran up to the car shortly after the car stopped. She tapped on the car in some manner (not sure if she hit the body of the driver's side or knocked on the glass on the driver's side). The noise caused the Black officer sitting on the passenger's side of the car to open fire. He shot the woman, and she died.

In March 2018, Mohamed Noor (the Black Minneapolis police officer involved in the incident) was charged with third-degree murder and second-degree manslaughter. At about the same time, he was fired from the Minneapolis Police Department. He was later found guilty as charged by a Minneapolis, Minnesota, court. I was very shocked at the outcome of this case. I think that many people in the Black community were equally shocked. Don't get me wrong; we definitely want to see police officers held accountable for wrongful murder/death. However, in some cases, there was a fine line, and this case seems to have met the fine-line guidelines.

Keep in mind, police officers oftentimes have to make a split-second decision, and not every time will that decision end up producing the best results. But in this case, I find the officer's actions understandable. The tap on the police car most likely caused fear and a quick response. I feel the biggest question in this case was that the police officer fired his weapon too quickly. According to media reports, the officer stated that he never saw the person and had no knowledge prior to the shooting of the victim's race or sex.

During the trial, Mr. Noor appeared to be remorseful and claimed his actions were a result of self-defense. I feel that he was genuinely sorry for his actions on that day, resulting in a loss of life, which I find is a rare quality in most police/law enforcement officers.

I really feel that this officer was unjustly charged and convicted in this case. First of all, who in their right mind would run up to an occupied police car and hit it. Based on my understanding, the incident occurred at night as well. That alone should have been enough justification for not proceeding to charge the officer with any charge of murder.

Secondly, I feel if Mr. Noor had shot and killed a Black or minority person, there would have been no murder charges filed against him. *The Intercept* news reported, "According to data compiled by the Star Tribune, Noor's case marks the first conviction out of 179 police-involved deaths in Minnesota since 2000." At best, in this case, a termination of Noor as a police officer should have been sufficient punishment for his actions, as deemed possibly being preventable.

In comparison to the Floyd George case, the Black Minneapolis police officer held his job until he was charged with murder by the county prosecutor's office. The White officer that killed Floyd was fired immediately after the tape of the incident was revealed.

However, it took over a week to get all four officers charged with murder by the Minneapolis county prosecutor's office. Many wonder if there would have been any criminal charges filed at all if it were not for people protesting all over the United States.

Now, we have to ask ourselves, why was this case handled so differently than the Noor case that preceded it? The case involving the Black officer followed most law enforcement protocols. Normally, the involved officer(s) is generally reassigned to desk duty while the matter is being investigated. Once the investigation is completed, then it is determined what if any charges or discipline will be administered.

The videotapes in the Floyd case were crystal clear that a handcuffed, restrained Black man was murdered by a White police officer's pressing his knee and body weight against Floyd's neck for approximately nine minutes. Floyd told the officers that he could not breathe and that he was hurting. Many people started gathering around, and many of these bystanders requested that the officer take his knee off Floyd's neck. Several people also shouted that the officer was killing Floyd, and if he did not stop the pressure on Floyd's neck, Floyd would die.

Even more alarming is that Floyd went lifeless after about six minutes of the knee pressure being applied to his neck. Even after he lay there lifeless, the officer continued to apply knee pressure to Floyd's neck for approximately three additional minutes. One can only assume that the officer wanted to make sure that Floyd was dead.

Even more disturbing is that when Officer Derek Chauvin (the officer who had his knee on Floyd's neck) was charged with murder and placed in jail, the media had reported that Chauvin, while in custody, should only be handled by White prison guards. What the hell is that about? So Black prison guards cannot be trusted to treat the White prisoner fairly. What about all the Black people that go to jail for committing similar crimes against White people? Should they all have been handled by prison guards of their own race as well?

To go a step further, if White people believe that a White prisoner would be treated unfairly by Black prison guards, then one would have to think that the reason that White people believe that a White person could not be treated fairly by Black prison guards is that they know that White guards do not treat Black inmates fairly.

Now, if a person ever had a reason to question our criminal justice system, there it is. The nerve of people to say or believe that institutionalized racism does not exist in the United States.

Which brings me to the Laquan McDonald case. I personally feel that the Chicago police killing of Laquan McDonald is what really started the Black Lives Matter movement. This is where a White Chicago police officer shot and killed a young Black man sixteen times. Just watching the videotape of the incident brings chills over your body.

Even more disturbing was watching each of the police officers at the trial giving their account of the events. To me, it was clear that all of them distorted the facts. The officer that shot McDonald stated that he feared for his life and that it was necessary to shoot the young black man sixteen times to neutralize the threat. It took sixteen shots to neutralize a threat from a young man carrying a street-legal knife walking down the street away from the police officer?

Equally disturbing is that nothing would have probably ever happened to the officer in this case if it were not for a reporter that insisted on seeing the dashcam footage of this shooting. Once the video footage was released to the public, only then did the officer get fired, arrested, and charged with murder. He was found guilty of sixteen counts of manslaughter and was sentenced to serve six years in jail.

I guess the good thing is that he did get some jail time. However, if I were to go in the middle of the street and shoot a dog sixteen times as the dog was just walking down the street, I would certainly get more than a six-year jail term. And we question, do Black lives matter? It would not matter if the dog was black, brown, white, gray, or any other color; it would not matter if the dog came from China, Germany, Japan, the United States, or any other country. Animal cruelty is animal cruelty. Why can't people be viewed in the same light? After all, any human life should at least be one notch above a dog's life. Human cruelty is human cruelty regardless of race, creed, sex, or color.

As far as I am concerned, this is a slap in the face to all Black people—six-year jail term for shooting a person who was walking away from him sixteen times. It was determined by the evidence that McDonald was no immediate threat to the officer. I guess I am more disturbed that the officer showed no remorse. During the hearing, the officer stated that he felt that his actions were necessary because he feared for his life and/or safety. The whole defense was nothing but one big lie after the next, which is usually the case when it comes to law enforcement criminal hearings.

It is clear that if the reporter had not insisted on viewing the videotapes of the shooting, there would not have been any criminal charges of trial. The whole incident would have just been swept under the rug, and the officer would have still been employed as a police officer. Wow, what does that say about our police department? And people have the nerve to wonder why Black people and minorities don't trust the police departments.

No sorrow, no regrets, no remorse, and no admission of wrongdoing before, during, or after the trial. According to Chauvin, he was just doing his job, doing what he had been trained to do. So if he were still a police officer, he could or would do the exact same thing again even after all evidence showed that his actions were wrong.

One needs to look no further than this case to see that the police training, accountability, and structure have to change. All law enforcement officials have to learn and respect the fact that all lives matter just as much as their lives do. Until then, there will never be equal justice for all people in the United States.

The two-tier system has got to stop. Americans have to start valuing nationality and not race. After all, how can people continue to go fight and die for a country, come back from war, and be treated like second-class citizens?

What America has always proclaimed is just one big lie—the "Star-Spangled Banner," "the land of the free and the home of the brave." Even at the time it was written, there were slaves in the United States. It makes me very angry today. When I look back at how we would say the pledge of allegiance in grammar school and singing the "Star-Spangled Banner" in school, never realizing that Black people never had the freedom and privileges that White people have had even to this very day. Even more disgusting, at the time, I believed the words to be true.

After spending over twenty years in background investigations, I am fully aware that Black, Brown, and White people all pretty much do the same things when growing up and/or living in similar environments. But history shows that it is not what people do that matters. What matters is who they are.

If people could only see some of the backgrounds of the judges, lawyers, and law enforcement personnel, not only would they be surprised, in some cases, they would be downright shocked to see some of the things that these people have done. History is full of cases that show racial injustices toward Black people. I chose to list a few recent cases to highlight my point. I feel that the following changes are necessary to the process of equal justice for all:

1. Totally revamp police training. Future police training has to teach officers how to:

   a. Value all life and that all lives matter exactly the same;
   b. Respect people's rights regardless of race, creed, color, or sex/sexual orientation;
   c. Treat all people as innocent until proven guilty, especially when the police did not observe the crime that is being alleged. This has to be reflected at all times to include when people are being investigated, charged, or suspected of a criminal involvement;
   d. Talk to all people with dignity and respect (even when they are not being respectful to law enforcement officers);
   e. Understand that their job as police officers is not to convict anyone of a crime;
   f. Understand that many people will react out of fear. Police officers need to address people's fears while attempting to make nonviolent arrests. Explain the

process and let people know that being arrested does not mean that they are guilty of a crime;

g. Return to community policing. Having certain police officers walking the neighborhood streets can be highly effective in reducing crime and restoring public trust. People are far more willing to cooperate with law enforcement officials that they know and trust;

h. Never discuss arrests or investigations of any criminal activity that is ongoing with the general public or the press;

i. Only shoot individuals as a last-resort option;

j. Have full body cam with voice and video during all arrests and/or investigations. This must have a strict enforcement policy. Failure to comply should result in immediate suspension or removal with possible jail time;

k. Realize that any officers caught lying during the investigative process should be subject to suspension or removal with possible jail time;

l. Understand that they will be held to the same accountability that is expected and required from the general public;

m. Fully value all human life and require that the use of mace, nightsticks, rubber bullets, and any other non-life threatening actions should always be the first line of defense to the greatest extent possible.

2. Any arrested person who claims that they were mistreated by police officers or were forced to make any confessions should be taken seriously.

a. All such incidents should be investigated by a separate investigative agency.

b. If allegations of police misconduct are found to be true, the officers involved should receive disciplinary action up to removal.

   c.   Police officers have to work hard to obtain public trust, and they must be made aware that they will be accountable for any wrongdoing.

3.   Courts need to restructure their current jury-selection procedures as follows:

   a.   Any minority should be given every opportunity to be tried by a jury where the majority of the jurors reflect the nationality of the person on trial. This is extremely important as many Whites don't know or understand what certain minorities face within their communities or environment.

   b.   To be fair, a jury should be made up of at least 75 percent of the same race as the defendant if possible. If not, it should be at least 75 percent minority (made up from other races when a Black or Brown person is being tried for a criminal offense).

   c.   For a court system to be fair to all races, it has to understand and accommodate for the various discrepant treatment that certain races receive within their communities.

By implementing most of the aforementioned policies and procedures, it will ensure that all people are receiving an equal justice system.

As one can see, the whole process will take a lot of time and effort, but the long-term effects will be phenomenal. It is about time that Black people as well as other minorities start getting equal and fair justice in our judicial system. The current system, as it is designed, is not and has never been totally fair to Blacks and Brown people.

We have to keep in mind that in 1776, the original constitution did not recognize Black people as US citizens who were equal to White US citizens, even though the US Constitution clearly stated that all men were created equal.

It really mystifies me as to why the United States always has had a problem recognizing Black people as equal to White people. I fail to understand how just being a slave would make a person less of a man or woman. In reality, they are still a man or woman just as any other man or woman. The only difference is the occupation, which certainly does not make them less of a human being.

Keep in mind that White people have also served as slaves (or in the case of White slavery, it is generally called indentured servants) in other countries. As a slave, Black people were denied rights because those rights and privileges were not granted to them as slaves. However, once the slaves were freed, they were supposed to be granted the same rights and privileges that any other citizen was entitled per the constitution.

So it appears that slavery is just used by White people as a cover-up to keep their hatred of Black people. There has to be something more than that. If slavery was the main issue between Black and White people, it would seem that Black people should be the ones that have bitterness toward White people. For the most part, Black people are not taught to have hatred of White people for the past enslavement of Black people.

Black people were stripped of their heritage and language when they became slaves. It does hurt when I see other races that migrated to the United States, and they still practice their native customs and language. Black people that were brought over as slaves were not entitled to the same privileges.

As descendants from slaves, we were stripped of everything including our identity. African Black people do not look at American-born Black people as part of the African race. They see us as Black people but not as Africans. So in essence, the American-born Blacks who are descendants of slaves are hybrid Black people. The purebred African-born Blacks see themselves as the true Black people.

If one takes a dog and used him as a servant to his master, once the service is ended for any reason, the dog is treated the same as any other dogs that were not used in the same manner. I use the dog as an example because it appears that in America, it easier to treat a dog with better respect and dignity than a Black person.

With all the things that the White race has done to Black people, we should be the ones that have a deep hatred for them, but ironically, we don't.

In our society, a white dog is treated no differently than a black or brown dog. Then why are Black and Brown people treated differently by White America?

When I was growing up, many people would tell me that most White people thought that they were superior to Black people. Even if White people thought that was true at that time, by now, they know that this is simply not true.

Did you know that I had a high school biology teacher tell me that Black people were inferior to White people? I responded, "How can that be true when Black people on average have a larger brain size than White people?" She replied that "a smaller brain works better than a larger brain because a fraction of the brain is only really fully utilized." Now who could have imagined such a thing? History has shown that when people, regardless of race, are provided the same environment and living conditions, they will produce similar results.

It is very hard to understand the level of hatred that Whites place on Blacks given the facts that most early Blacks were brought to the United States against their will. They were enslaved, degraded, and mistreated at no real fault of their own. Even more interesting is that most Blacks who were born of slaves who are in the United States today do not have pure African blood. I would go as far as to say that 100 percent of the American Blacks who were descended from slaves have White blood in their veins.

With this being the case, how can Whites still have such a strong dislike for Black people? For some reason, Whites do not want to acknowledge this fact. Maybe this will help people better understand what I am talking about. In America, it is an insult to be half Black and half White. Under these circumstances, a child could look Black, White, or mixed (which is usually brown). However, a person born of a 100 percent African and a 100 percent Anglo-Saxon (white) must consider themselves as a Black person. They can claim mixed race; however, in America, mixed race between a Black and White person means they are Black. If this is not the case, then why is there no spot on applications that lists your race as mixed race?

If a person is half Mexican and half White, they can claim Mexican or White as their race. If a person is half Chinese and half White, they can claim Chinese or White as their race. There is no exception. Anyone mixed with Black is Black. Why is it that when Black blood is mixed with white blood, the only acceptable race of that person in America is Black?

To show how ridiculous this is, when a person gets a blood transfusion, no one knows if the blood that they are getting is from a White person or a Black person, which means if the White person gets Black blood during the blood transfusion process, then he too is Black. Hopefully, people can begin to see how ridiculous the whole process is? Black is Black when it is convenient to Whites.

Just on the reasons above, one can see that there *is* systemic racism in America. Any White person who fails to recognize that systemic racism in America has to be a racist. America *needs* to stop playing and wake up and recognize that this is a *real* racial problem in the United States. After all, the only way that you can really fix a problem is you first have you recognize that a problem exists.

As I see it, institutional racism in America begins at birth. Why is there a need to put race on a birth certificate? For all Americans born in the United States, the only designation of citizenship should be American. There is absolutely no reason whatsoever to identify race as Black or White on a birth certificate.

The only possible reason that I can think of is to keep a racial division. I feel that institutionalized racism will only begin to be wiped out in America when they stop putting race on the birth certificate or on any other legal document or employment applications.

Another big problem for Black and Brown men is the elevation of juveniles to adults in certain criminal offenses. When I was young and did not know better, I thought that it was fair to elevate a juvenile to an adult if the crime warranted it. I soon realized that this was a brainwashing tool. I see this as a very critical problem in the United States for the following reasons: First of all, Black and Brown males are the primary targets under the provisions of elevating juveniles to adults. So why was this ever implemented in the first place? My best guess is to put juveniles away for life or to be able to legally execute a juvenile of certain crimes that meet a so-called criteria.

I now see this policy for what it is: pure garbage. A juvenile is a juvenile; a child is a child; an adult is an adult—or is he? America has a real problem when it comes to defining an adult.

This policy creates a huge double standard. Under this policy, the only way that a person could be elevated to an adult status is that he has to commit a crime so bad that it would automatically make him an adult; therefore, he should receive the punishment of an adult up to and including the death penalty.

There is too much confusion as to exactly when you are an adult in the United States. In some states, you can drink alcohol at eighteen years of age, but most states require you to be twenty-one years of age. In some states, you can smoke cigarettes at eighteen years of age, and some states require that you be twenty-one years of age.

I am a firm believer that there should be one age that makes a person an adult in the United States. And once they become an adult, they are granted all entitlements that any adults are entitled to have. For example, if you are an adult at eighteen years of age, then you should be able to buy alcohol and smoke cigarettes and have any rights and privileges that any other adult has. Right now, in some states, you can and some you cannot.

What makes this even a bigger problem is that in all fifty states, you can join the armed forces, which means that you can die for your country at eighteen years old, and you can be charged in a court of law as an adult. Moreover, you can get married at eighteen years old in all fifty states, have a family, live independently, and be financially self-supportive, but you still cannot drink alcohol or smoke cigarettes in some states. This just does not make rational sense. In some places, you are fully grown at eighteen, some at twenty-one. There should be one universal grown adult age in the United States. To me, if you can get married, raise a family, live independently, and join the armed forces, you should be an adult in all fifty states.

Right now, the only way to elevate any juvenile to an adult is sentence him to a crime. This policy has been overturned for the criminal justice system to be fair to all people. Let's take a critical look at this policy.

- Most people directly affected by this program are Black and Brown males.
- The only real purpose of this program is to elevate young Black and Brown people to adulthood for the sole purpose of executing them or giving them a long-term to life prison sentence.
- The only winner with this program is the system that designed and created it to further criminalize Black, Brown, and other minorities.
- It is absolutely ludicrous that the only way that a juvenile can be elevated to an adult is to convict him of a crime that the criminal justice system feels should be punishable as an adult.
- This methodology defies all laws of human nature as the only way to elevate a juvenile to being an adult is to try them as an adult, including being independent, having a family, being self-supportive, or serving in the US Military, which makes absolutely no sense when a person can go into the armed forces and die for this country but cannot be considered an adult and unable to enjoy all the rights and privileges that a twenty-one-year-old does.
- If a person cannot be elevated to an adult for the possibility of giving his life to this county, it shows that there is clearly something wrong with this policy. Anyone willing to make the ultimate sacrifice for their country should be extended all the rights and privileges for any full-grown adult.

For all of the above reasons, I truly feel that eliminating the elevation of juveniles to adults based on a criminal offense would be a giant step in the equal process of all people.

Let's take a critical look at the definition of a juvenile. *Webster's Dictionary* defines a juvenile as a young person. I would further define *juvenile* as "a young maturing person that has not reached full adulthood."

The United States Criminal Justice System views eighteen years of age as an adult. Therefore, under normal circumstances, anyone who commits a crime at the age of eighteen or older is charged as an adult, which means that crimes committed by anyone under the age of eighteen are considered juvenile crimes and are handled in a juvenile court. However, the prosecutors have the right to partition the courts to have a juvenile tried as an adult for a crime or criminal act that fits some type of predetermined profile.

I personally feel that no juvenile should ever be elevated to an adult because of a crime that was committed while he was a juvenile. In our society, under no other circumstances can a juvenile be elevated to an adult regardless of how good, responsible, or adult a behavior they display. For example, you can have a juvenile working and making the same amount of money as an adult. However, he cannot live or do the same things that an adult can do, including the following:

- He cannot buy a car on credit without a cosigner.
- He cannot rent an apartment without a cosigner.
- He cannot buy a house without a cosigner.
- He cannot have a credit card without a cosigner.
- He cannot get married without a cosigner.
- He cannot join the armed forces without a cosigner.

Let's take a look at a case that was previously known as the DC sniper killings. This is a case that involved a juvenile Lee Boyd Malvo and his adult stepfather, John Allen Muhammad. Together, they shot and killed a number of people in the Washington, DC, area. When they were caught and charged, the judicial system charged Malvo (the juvenile) as an adult; he was approximately fifteen or sixteen years old at the time.

Now, anyone looking at this case would know that the adult stepfather was directly responsible for the actions of the juvenile. The juvenile was under the responsibility of the stepfather, which leads to the question, how could this juvenile be charged as an adult when he was a child that was totally or partially dependent on his stepfather for survival?

In this case, the stepfather should be totally responsible for the juvenile's actions; the juvenile was totally dependent on the stepfather for support. It is certainly clear that if it were not for the actions of the stepfather, the juvenile would not have been involved in such activity.

There are a number of reasons that a juvenile commits a criminal act, including some of the following:

- They have some type of mental disability.
- They have behavior-related issues.
- They have issues stemming from teaching, training, or social environment.

Whatever the reason, a juvenile is still a juvenile and should be acknowledged as such throughout the criminal justice system.

Most adults will agree that they were not fully mentally developed mentally as a juvenile. From my own experience, I did not fully understand death and dying as a juvenile, but it was easy to understand life and living. I had no concept of the entire scope of dying and/or death. Therefore, I could never fear death because I did not understand it. I was in my early twenties when I realized anybody can die, including myself, and that life is to be valued. This is when I realized the value of human life.

A young mind can easily be swayed by adults, environment, and media. In most cases, most juveniles are just not fully capable of making 100 percent rational decisions. Even as a young adult, I made poor decisions that could have resulted in criminal charges. Oftentimes, I did not fully understand the ramifications of my actions until after I committed the act.

I really believe that our society is a major factor in juvenile misbehavior. For the most part, we really don't teach our children at early ages about crime and criminal activity, including the possible long-term ramifications. I strongly recommend having ethics classes for all children in elementary school to start somewhere around the third- or fourth-grade levels. People need to learn society's values and expectations at an early age. For example, if a child is around other children growing up who are stealing and promoting this behavior, that child may start and continue that behavior up until some point in his life when he realizes this is not correct behavior. Some may learn too late and end up in jail or worse. It was not until my second year in college that I had any ethics classes. Learning ethics was one of the best things that could have happened to me in my life. In fact, it may have saved me from serving jail time or dying from violence in the streets.

Our current society does not properly prepare our young children with the tools that are necessary to promote a society of full awareness of what is right and what is wrong. Even so, some teaching and training have to be learned through life experience. No one can fully appreciate life until they fully understand death.

For those reasons, I feel that no juvenile should ever be elevated to an adult. There are too many factors that have to be considered in elevating a juvenile to an adult, the greatest factor being life. There is no way that a juvenile can ever have the experience necessary to be considered as an adult. The mere fact that a juvenile has never been or could ever be totally independent should more than suffice as evidence.

Another factor that complicates young children's understanding of what is right and what is wrong is media (mostly television). I really feel that television can have a negative impact on an underdeveloped mind.

America has got to come to the realization that a juvenile can never be an adult; that is why he is a juvenile until he becomes an adult. I understand that certain crimes make a society want to implement harsher punishments. However, not even a parent can treat their juvenile children as an adult. A parent will go to jail for disciplining a child as though he was an adult. There were times that I would have liked to have fought my teenage son as an adult man. I did not do that because he was not a man. I respected the fact that he was not an adult man, and I did not want to go to jail for possible child abuse. Just as a parent has to respect the rights of a juvenile, so must the justice system.

Society has failed our youth. It is time that we realize that as a nation and take the necessary steps to correct this. *The double standard for juveniles must end!*

Final Analysis

My work, education, and life experience as a Black man have led me to conclude that our criminal justice system is not fair to Black, Brown, and other minorities primarily because it was never really designed to be fair to all. Keep in mind that in 1776, when the constitution was drafted and implemented for the United States, Black people were not even considered as citizens, which means there is no way that the laws, policies, and procedures could be administered fairly to them. For example, prior to the 1990s, the police, while conducting a traffic stop on a Black individual, would tell him to "get out the car, nigga." How can anyone justify this gross injustice to Black people? No other race in the United States had to endure such demoralizing treatment. Under those circumstances, how can any law enforcement officer say that they treat everybody the same? No other race had to endure the humiliation of being called racial slag names when they were asked to get out of their cars.

Prior to the 1990s, it was common for White people to call Black people "niggas" at any time for any reason. It is really hard to understand why in the twenty-first century there is such a great divide between Black and White people, especially when you consider the fact that most of the Black race that was brought to America as slaves; their offspring are no longer purebred Africans. Today, I really don't think that you would be able to find any 100 percent pure-blooded African-Americans that were children born of slaves.

So with that in mind, there is White blood flowing in all Black people that are descendants of slaves. White people have got to wake up and face that fact that all or most Black people today who were descendants of slaves are of mixed race. America has totally destroyed the Black race that was descended from slaves. They tainted our blood and destroyed our race and culture. Then they have the nerve to treat Black people like we are different when in essence we are actually a part of them.

Before we can begin to move forward to mend fences, everybody has to understand and face the mistakes of the past. We have to realize that all people really are created equal and that everyone is entitled to equal and fair treatment. This has to be taught in our schools, churches, employments, laws, and justice systems.

Base on my life experience, I just don't feel a training class can make real change. America has to restructure its entire teaching and training systems, including...

Education. All schools need to focus on equality of all people. They need to instill that skin color means nothing and that all people's insides are the same. This should be a relatively easy process to accomplish. If one were to take a black dog and a white dog and make a comparison, one would see that the only difference is the color of their fur. I truly believe if people can treat all dogs equally, they can do the same with people.

Employment. All employers have to value diversity. They must practice being fair for all employees. All promotions have to be based on education, experience, and accomplishments. When all applicants are basically equal in qualifications, then companies need to look at which candidate would contribute to the company's having a good, diverse, fair workforce. For example, if 90 percent of a company's workforce is male, this may be a great opportunity to select a female.

Discrimination in employment is real. When I was a federal employee, I used to hear managers say education should not matter in promotions. I asked a few people to explain why they felt that way. The basic answer that I generally received was that a person could not get a degree in the type of employment that they were doing. Any educated person would realize that this philosophy is ridiculous.

Higher education brings better reading/writing, speaking, and analytical skills.

I later realized that most of the higher-level managers working at most companies during that time did not have a college education. At that point, I understood their reasoning, which was, "Let's keep our promotion system the same," which would not allow credit for education. Furthermore, what would be the sense of anybody's getting any additional higher-level education if it is not going to make a difference in their employment career or advancement opportunities.

Police Departments. The current and past culture has been so bad. Unfortunately, I just don't think that they can be salvaged. The current system needs to be scrapped and reconstructed from the ground up.

Suggestions

A revised police officer training program should have a primary focus on all lives matter regardless of race. Police have to understand that their primary job is to serve and protect. They are not to judge or to make people guilty. While investigating a crime, they are to disclose everything involved in the investigation, including all witness statements and other findings that may or may not support the proposed evidentiary record. As it has turned out in so many cases, that one witness statement or piece of evidence that don't fit the puzzle turns out in fact to be the right statement or piece of evidence.

Impartial investigations are the most effective way of obtaining the whole truth. Police departments should not be making any decisions of innocence or guilt based on their findings. They should turn their findings over to the legal department for analysis and advice on how to proceed.

Police officers have to be made aware that if it is found that they intentionally misrepresented any evidentiary record, they will be fined, fired, suspended, and/or prosecuted. Police have to start being held totally accountable and responsible for their actions.

Because police can take a life at any time base on their discretion, they all need to be licensed and held to licensing standards and requirements, which means if they are found guilty of violating rules, laws, and/or procedures, their license can be revoked and that they would never be able to hold the police officer position in any state of the United States. Currently, police officers have very little accountability for their actions. Future police officers have to be held fully accountable for their actions.

The current culture of most of the police departments is that you don't "rat" on a fellow police officer, which means if another officer observes an officer violating policy, the officer observing the policy violation would turn a blind eye. They will even testify or provide statements in the defense of the officer's criminal activity. This culture can no longer continue if there is to ever be total integrity within the police departments. It is currently costing states, cities, and the federal departments millions of dollars in lawsuits.

The country has got to realize that there are serious problems within our police departments. Many officers have been promoted or given raises or recognition for criminal acts in closing criminal cases. This is most evident in charging innocent people of crimes that they did not commit to close a case.

I currently have a hard time understanding the many police officers that shoot and kill a person, especially when deadly force was not required or necessary, having no remorse for the life that they took. Oftentimes, many police officers state that they were just during their jobs. To me, even if deadly force is deemed necessary, there should be some remorse. After all, somebody's life has just been taken. There's certainly nothing wrong with apologizing for taking someone's life and expressing that they wish that it has been some alternative. A good police officer has to value all life regardless of race or crime committed.

Moreover, even if I shot a home intruder, I would still be remorseful that I took someone's life. Although the shooting may be justified, human life should still be held to a higher regard.

Currently, police officers are trained to shoot to kill. This policy has to change. Future police officers need to be trained to access a situation and to use force as necessary to defuse the situation. Therefore, a life-threatening situation should always be the last alternative.

Police have to understand that just because a person runs from the police does not mean that they are guilty of any crime and should not be shot. If a person is running away from a police officer even if the police officer says stop, if there is no reason to suspect that the person committed a crime, the person should not be shot at. Running away from a law enforcement official is not a reason to take a person's life in and of itself. I am of the belief that a police officer should only shoot at a person that they have personally witnessed the crime or that the crime is currently in progress.

Another thing that needs to be seriously looked at is police on-duty hours and work schedules. Many police officers are currently working twelve-hour shifts. On top of that, they are working two and three additional jobs. This makes absolutely no sense to me. Twelve-hour shifts are too many hours to work on a consistent basis. On some occasions, they have to work overtime, which could be up to fourteen to sixteen hours a day.

It does not take a rocket scientist to know that the more hours that people work, the less alert they are. There is absolutely no way that most people can stay or be fully alert working twelve-hour shifts on a consistent basis. I remember watching the officer's trial during the Laquan McDonald case during televised proceedings. When the involved officer took the stand, he stated that prior to reporting to his Chicago police employment, he had worked another job (I can't remember the total amount of hours that he said he worked the other job, but I think he said six hours).

I really believe that the long hours that police are working are affecting their alertness, responsiveness, and judgment. It is well known that when people are tired, they make bad judgment calls, which can cause a situation to escalate unnecessarily, which can end in an unjustified life-or-death situation. I would recommend that twelve-hour work schedules be abolished. Due to the nature and stress of their job, they should be limited to an eight-hour work schedule as much as possible. It is understandable that overtime will be necessary in emergency situations. However, every effort should be made to keep police officers working as few hours as possible.

Another thing, I feel that police officers should never work two jobs. Most of the police officers that I have met all moonlight and have one or more other employment activities while also being full-time police officers. Most police officers make a decent living wage and should be capable of living a decent life with their regular salary and overtime opportunities. Police officers should be alert as much as possible when scheduled to work.

Finally, I feel that the training, hiring, and selecting of police officers need to be regulated by the federal government. Every agency should have the same training and hiring procedures. Police should have extensive psychological training and evaluations. They must have rigorous background investigations, including interviewing grammar, high and college school teachers, and former classmates. Every effort needs to be made to make sure that future police officers are of sound mind and that they have had no known racial or cultural issues/problems.

More than any other profession, police officers have the ultimate decision to determine a life or death situation. Therefore, I would suggest that they be licensed just as doctors, lawyers, etc. are. And if it is determined that a police officer's license is to be suspended or revoked, then the police officer can no longer work as a law enforcement official in any city, state, or federal agency.

These changes are necessary to bring accountability, fairness, and public trust among all people, genders, and races. This will be a long but necessary process. Only when the police departments and law enforcement agencies have been totally reformed to operate on honesty and integrity will they gain the public trust of all people. This will be the first time in the United States history that law enforcement will be totally fair for all people. In return, people and communities will be more cooperative in working with law enforcement agencies and assisting in their investigations.

America has got to change and stop lying to itself. There is a serious racial problem that exists in the United States. We the people have to recognize it and deal with it. Through experience, I can say the worst thing a person can go through in life is to be the same as any other human being but yet be treated differently.

Finally, I have to mention some of the events that have occurred under a recent past president. This president ran under the slogan "MAKE AMERICA GREAT AGAIN," also referred to as "MAGA." The problem with the slogan is with the word "again." Once you say *again*, you have to go back to a time when America was great. Well, most Americans feel that America has always been great but has had a very dark past with racism, slavery, and sexism. So it leads one to wonder if what is truly being referenced here is to go back to a time in America where none of those factors mattered because White men were considered to be the dominant and controlling force in America.

This president would frequently make references to being the least racist person ever and to state that no other president since former president Abraham Lincoln has done more for Back people. My question is what the hell has he done? I can see nothing that his presidency has done that would make him stand out as making outstanding contributions to Black Americans.

In fact to the contrary, this president has brought the greatest divide between Black and White people that I have ever seen in my lifetime. This president has never supported any Black Lives Matter movements and refused to recognize that America has an issue with institutionalized racism, which is a direct slap in the face to any Black American.

He outwardly supported White nationalist groups and condoned police violence against Black people. This president supported confederate flags on government premises, keeping statues of confederate leaders on federal government property, and naming of federal military bases after Confederate war leaders.

Keep in mind, this is the twenty-first century. Who would expect such behavior in this day and age from a commander in chief?

It is interesting that this president, while campaigning for president, went to Michigan, Pennsylvania, and Wisconsin and asked Black voters to give him a chance. He stated to the Black voters, "What do you have to lose?" further emphasizing that the previous

Democratic presidents have done little to nothing to elevate Black interests.

The final outcome of the election in November 2016 was that this president won the election by winning Michigan, Pennsylvania, and Wisconsin (all three of these states were expected to overwhelmingly vote Democratic in the presidential election). So it would appear that the Black people in these states decided to take this presidential candidate at his word and gave him a chance.

Well, guess what—he lied. He did nothing to provide any assistance to progress the betterment of Black and Brown people. Under his leadership, I would say the United States actually went backward. Race relations appeared to go back to the 1950s. The racial tensions rose so high, it was almost at Civil War levels.

This president condoned White supremacist groups and failed to recognize any Black Lives Matter movements and failed to speak against the police violence on Black and Brown citizens. This president had the nerve to even say that he was not a racist and that no other president in modern-day history has done more for Black people than him.

The Black and Brown population in the United States has become accustomed to being lied to by politicians promising to bring real change in racial equality. However, it is an unforgivable insult to stand before America and state that you have done so much for Black people. When in reality, this president has done virtually nothing to improve Black and Brown economic equality in the United States.

When are people in America going to realize that Black people are not stupid? This former president had stood before the American people and stated that he was so proud of his record in filling over three hundred vacant federal judge positions. However, he failed to mention that not one of the appointed judges was Black. Can anyone believe in the twenty-first century that over three hundred vacancies were filled and not one Black person was assigned to any of these positions? *What an absolute disgrace.* Now, this is coming from a person that proclaims that he does not have a racist bone in his body.

White America has got to learn that it is not what you say but what you do that counts. Black people can smell racism a mile away.

Words mean nothing. Black and Brown people are tired of lies and idle promises. You do not have to stand and tell Black people that you are not a racist. Actions speak louder than words. Black people will be the first ones to tell you when your actions are not racist.

With that being said, these same states that gave the then presidential candidate a chance took it away from him in the 2020 presidential election. This president then went around stating that he could not understand why he lost the 2020 election and that there had to be some type of fraud. It is clear to any rational person why this president lost the 2020 election: when given the chance that he asked for, he did nothing. *Now guess what, Mr. President. You paid the price for doing nothing.*

But even worse than doing nothing, he was adamant that he did a whole lot. Today is a different day than in the past. When you slap people today, you just might get slapped back tomorrow.

Moreover, what followed was a disaster. This president failed to accept the outcome of the 2020 election and spread lies that the election results in Pennsylvania, Michigan, and Wisconsin were fraudulent. At the time that this then candidate for president won the election, these three states were expected to overwhelmingly vote for the Democratic presidential nominee. Therefore, the democratic candidate did not campaign heavily in those states.

In a smart move, the Republican Party took advantage of lack of Democratic campaigning in those three states, and it paid off. The Republican presidential candidate won the presidency with the win in those states. The former president made numerous unsuccessful legal attempts to overturn the election results in these three states.

The biggest mistake he made was underestimating the voters in those three states. He made a campaign promise that he did not keep. While campaigning, he asked the voters in those states to give him a chance. He specifically addressed the fact that the Democratic Party always make promises to the Black community and never deliver. He went so far as to state to the Black voters, "What do you have to lose?"

After this man was elected, he answered the question really quickly. Under this president, the Black race stood to lose everything. This man did absolutely nothing to advance racial equality in the

United States. I would even go as far as to say that his presidency set the racial divide in the United States back to the 1950s (that is as far back as I can remember).

This president did absolutely nothing to benefit the Black race as a whole. As president, he never denounced White supremacy groups. He supported groups carrying Nazi and confederate flags. To make matters worse, he would get on national television and tell that world that he was the least racist person in the world. *Mr. President, if you are the least racist person in the world, I would hate to see the most racist person in the world.*

The real reason that this president lost his reelection was that he failed to deliver on his promises to work hard for all people and to mend the divide. One thing that this presidency proved is just how divided our country is. During his failed reelection attempt, he lost the election with the highest number of votes than any elected president had previously been elected by in the history of the United States. Which means one thing: that about half the American people either love or support this former president's policies and or procedures on racial divide.

At least the world knows now what America is really all about; racism runs rampant here. What's ironic is White people are proud to stick their chests out and savor the fact that in America there is something called White privilege, which is something all White people enjoy being Americans.

So what does White privilege mean? I am not White, so I cannot answer that question for what it means to White people. But I can answer what it means to me as a Black man. To me, being White privileged means that no matter what Black persons accomplish—be it monetary, status, or position—they will always be considered as less than a White person regardless of the White person's money, status, or position because White people have something that no Black person could ever have, and that is the privilege of being White.

Maybe that is the real reason why a person, no matter how much White blood that they have at birth, is always considered Black. Under no circumstances will America give any human being mixed with Black the privilege of being able to claim White privilege.

One thing for sure is that this deeply divided racism cannot continue in the United States. We can no longer continue to grow as a nation if we keep the current divide. I cannot understand why this is a hard task for White America when all they have to do is follow the principles that this nation was founded on. It is right in the constitution: all men are created equal.

Today, we all know that that language has always been a lie in America. A word to the wise is that America has got to wake up and start doing the right thing. America can begin by accepting the fact that all so-called Black Americans that were born in the United States from descendants of slaves are not really Black Americans. They are really mixed Americans. That is right! White blood is running through all of our veins, which means we are not all Black as White America would like us to be. To be fair to the so-called Black Americans, future birth certificates of all American-born children should only display the child's nationality and no longer include race.

White America has nobody to blame for this fiasco but themselves. They always perpetuated how much they hate Black people while Black people were getting lighter and lighter. Evidentially, Black people were not hated as badly as they wanted people to think.

Black people are known for not sticking together when compared to all other races. I personally feel the reason Black people have a hard time sticking together is because during slavery, the slaves were separated to make every effort to keep them away from other slaves who spoke the same language, which made it difficult for the slaves to communicate with each other, and they had to learn English to communicate effectively with one another.

Just as White men created this situation among Black people, they are going to face another problem in the future. Black people are going to learn how to unite and stick together as all the other races do. And when that happens, it is going to be another problem that White America is going to have to deal with. Black people are not going to continue to accept the second-class citizenship that they have been forced to live with in America.

As hard as it is to believe, most Black people do not hate White people. We just want to be treated with the same dignity and respect as they are. I guarantee if you were to ask most Black people if they had to do it all over again, would they prefer to be Black or White, most would respond that they still would want to be Black. Isn't that amazing after everything that Black people have faced as a race in America? We appreciate who we are. We don't appreciate how we are treated.

America has to come to the realization that there really is a serious racial problem in America. If steps are not taken in the near future to deal with this problem, it is going to turn into a nightmare. History has shown that when people are treated differently, they act differently. Oftentimes, it results in the behavior that the level of treatment was designed to do. For example, if you keep telling a child that she is never going to be anything and telling another child that they are expected to be highly successful, it generally works out that the one child has low self-esteem and tends to be less successful than the child that is told she will be successful and is expected to be successful.

This two-tier system and double standard have got to stop, which is the only way that America is going to fully reach the success that it needs to continue to be a great nation. Failing to recognize when change is necessary then doing nothing is only setting America up for failure. I only hope that America does not suffer the fate that so many great nations faced in the past. America has to use history in its favor as no nation has ever remained great forever.

For a nation to truly remain great, it has to recognize its strengths and weaknesses and act accordingly. The future greatness of America depends on America's ability to unite all of its citizens. America has to stop making excuses and stand up for what is right and what America truly embodies: justice and equality for all.

I am further amazed at the many White Americans who do not think or admit that there is institutionalized racism in America. If there was ever any doubt, one needs to look no further than the storming-of-the-capitol event on January 6, 2021. This incident was a violent attack by supporters of a former president in an attempt to overturn a presidential election result. This was the day that congress was certifying the electoral vote for a newly elected president. On this day, the outgoing president held a rally to express his anger and disbelief of losing a reelection majority vote.

This outgoing president held a rally in Washington, DC. At the end of the rally, this president directed the crowd to go down to the capitol and protest against the certification of the electoral vote process. When the crowd got to the Capitol, they turned violent. The crowd overrode the capitol police and entered the US Capitol, looking for the speaker of the house and the vice president at the time.

According to news media reports, only one person was shot and killed by a Capitol police officer. It is understandable that the Capitol police did not shoot because they were severely outnumbered. However, about a couple of months earlier, there was a Black Lives Matter rally in the same location. In addition to having a large capitol police presence, there were probably thousands of National Guard soldiers to protect the US Capitol and the White House.

On January 6, 2021, most of the crowd were angry supporters of the former president. Many of these protesters were known to be or have violent tendencies. The racial makeup of these protesters was probably 99 percent White.

Due to a severe lack of law enforcement officials, the crowd entered the Capitol. There is no way that this crowd should have been able to enter the Capitol. The only way that the crowd was able to get away with this activity was because of their race. There is absolutely no way that a primarily Black racial-makeup crowd would have gotten away with storming the capitol. I am confident that if a primarily Black crowd would have attempted to unlawfully enter the capitol, there would have been a lot of dead Black bodies.

To me, this was one of the worst embarrassments to our US Government as government officials failed to adequately protect members of the House of Representative and the Senate. The only way that this crowd was allowed to penetrate the Capitol was because of the racial makeup of the crowd. There is no other group of people that could have pulled that off.

Therefore, without question, this incident in and of itself clearly showed that only White lives matter in the United States. This was an on-purpose institutional failure to protect a primarily White race group. This was truly a sad event as the federal government protected one so-called White-privileged group at the expense of another White-privileged group. The point that I am trying to make is that *no Black racial group* would have ever been allowed to unlawfully enter the Capitol under any circumstances—*ever*.

There currently is a Black Lives Matter movement going on in the United States. This is a very serious issue that has to be dealt with. Based on my observations, Black lives don't matter in the United States because Black lives were never meant to matter in the United States.

To validate this point, most people are not aware that a White person has never been put to death for killing a Black person no matter how heinous the crime. This fact alone is proof positive that there is only one race's life that matters in the United States. Now that hurts.

Some lawmakers had been discussing reparations for Black people that were descendants of slaves. Honestly, America, the *best* reparation that America can give Black people is *to give us the same treatment* that they give *White* people. That is all we want! Then we will be able to make our own money. Just open up the doors, and we will get it ourselves. "Liberty and justice for all"—*really*, America?

The primary reason that I wrote this book is to shed light on a broken criminal justice system that desperately needs changing. The United States became an independent country in 1776. At that time, most Black people were slaves and were not looked at as citizens the same as White people were. Keeping that in mind, if the system was not designed to include Black people as equal citizens, then it was never totally fair and just to Black people even to this day.

As of the writing of this book (2021), we are still having high racial tensions and racial divide in the United States. I only hope that one day, my children and their children will see a fair and just America, one that will respect all lives and treat people the same.

Man up, America, and finally *do the right thing*. The only way that we are truly going to grow and maintain greatness is *together*. One old saying that is so true: "United we stand and divided we fall." If America does not address this necessary evil (take a note from history), *we will fail.*

Despite all that I have witnessed, felt, and endured in this life, I am hopeful that life, liberty, and the pursuit of happiness will eventually finally prevail. I live for the day that Black, Brown, and White are all privileged. Our future success will be dependent on being *una faccia, una razza* (one face, one race)!

Finally, I would like to address the Black Lives Matter movement: I feel that the Black Lives Matter movement is currently misunderstood by many in the White American community.

The Black Lives Matter movement is a movement to spotlight the injustices of Black and Brown Americans. These injustices are real, and show that there is a double standard in America's criminal justice system.

It is ironic that many White Americans, when asked what they think about the Black Lives Matter movement, quickly respond with "all lives matter". While this sounds like a respectable answer, we all know that this is really not true.

Without a doubt, I think the best answer to the question "do Black lives matter in America" is *"Yes, but just not as much as White lives matter."*

One needs to look no further than the sentencing of Derek Chauvin—twenty two and a half years for a modern day lynching of a Black man. Which to me, is a downright disgrace. Chauvin was a sworn peace officer who was supposed to serve and protect all the people that he was sworn to serve and protect. Moreover, he knew exactly what he was doing. This was no accident. Mission accomplished Chauvin.

Georgy Floyd's death cost America billions of dollars. Yet his killer gets a twenty two and a half years sentence. The reality here is that America will bar no expense to spare a White life when guilty of a Black or Brown death. America, is this really Blind Justice?

Come on America, face the truth—Blind Justice does not exist in America, nor has it ever existed in America.

ABOUT THE AUTHOR

Terry Nelson grew up in Chicago, Illinois, and spent most of his adult life in suburban Chicago locations. He has a Bachelor of Arts degree, a Bachelor of Science degree, a Master of Public Administration degree, and a Law degree. His employments include twenty-five years of US government service, twenty years of US government contract employment, and over ten years of teaching part-time college courses.

CPSIA information can be obtained
at www.ICGtesting.com
Printed in the USA
BVHW051224161122
652120BV00001B/57